Crisis and conscience in the Middle East

Crisis and conscience in the Middle East

by Christian E. Hauer, Jr.
Introduction by Senator Hugh Scott
Chicago · Quadrangle Books · 1970

Library of Congress Catalog Card Number: 70-108445

"Blessed are the peacemakers, for they shall be called sons of God."

JESUS THE CHRIST
MATTHEW 5:9

"Be disciples of Aaron, loving peace and pursuing peace, loving mankind and drawing them to the Teaching."

HILLEL THE ELDER
MISHNAH ABOTH 1:12

"Fight in the way of Allah against those who fight against you, but begin not hostilities. Lo! Allah does not love aggressors."

MUHAMMED
THE KORAN 2:190

Contents

Introduction

Senator Hugh Scott

In this essay which he offers "in the hope that it may encourage more people to join the quest for a humane resolution of the Middle East crisis," Christian Hauer has tried to be objective. Committed neither to the cause of Jew nor Arab, but only to the overriding interest of humanity, he has studied the question in depth and at firsthand, both as a humanitarian and as a theologian. But in the process he has reached the conclusion that peace in the Middle East depends on the Arabs' willingness to recognize the existence of Israel and to reach a settlement. The details of the settlement are secondary.

In reaching this conclusion, Dr. Hauer expresses his own profound convictions—that Israel has the same right to sovereign existence as any other nation; that the people of

Israel have the right to live free from the threat of genocide; and that the military actions taken by Israel in her own defense are justified by the threats and belligerent actions taken against her.

To the prejudiced or ill-informed these may not appear to be "objective" statements of belief, however obvious they may appear to those of us who have followed the uneasy childhood of Israel from her painful birth through her twentieth birthday. That is because it is virtually impossible to be coldly objective in a situation in which one side preaches genocide and revenge while the other struggles for a chance to live and asks for nothing better than peace with its neighbors.

We have already witnessed genocide in this generation, and those who thought it an idle threat or Zionist propaganda thirty years ago have lived to regret their silence and their inaction while Hitler systematically carried out his nefarious plan for the "final solution of the Jewish question."

I wholeheartedly support Dr. Hauer when he calls for action now—before it is too late. "Time grows short," he writes, "and we never had too much to begin with. . . . The match is to the fuse, and not all of the world's powder is stored in a distant corner of the Mediterranean." To genocide, then, is added the danger of spreading world conflict. To humane considerations are added political expediency and the very survival of twentieth-century civilization as the Great Powers lock horns in the Middle East.

But neither Dr. Hauer as a theologian nor I as a politician preach appeasement of the Arabs or their Soviet allies in the hope of averting such a conflict. We seek a peaceful and equitable solution, an honorable settlement for both sides which is the only true basis for a lasting peace, a settlement freely arrived at by the parties concerned and not imposed from the outside.

Israel is willing to discuss such a settlement. But when will the Arab leaders be willing to meet the leaders of a state whose existence they deny? Until they are, and so long as they insist on a state of war, and so long as they encourage their terrorists to attack, there should be no more pressure on Israel to yield a single inch of territory and expose her people to further aggression. There should be no more pressure on Israel to accept Arab threats, boycotts, blockades, and terrorism as something normal and reasonable, and to refrain from counteraction.

The year 1969 saw tensions heightening and an increase in Arab terrorist activity, bringing with it the greater involvement of countries such as Lebanon that had attempted to remain aloof, antagonizing neither Arabs nor Israelis. Every day there are new accounts of attack and counterattack, terrorist incursions and retaliatory measures, to such an extent that they now become a commonplace part of the news. But every time an announcer states that five or ten Israelis have been killed, one must remember that Israel's entire standing army consists of fifteen thousand or sixteen thousand men—less than the complement of one United States infantry division. With a population of 2,600,000, the loss of one man is equivalent to that of ten in a country like Egypt where population is ten times greater, or to one hundred in the United States. As the author points out, the 200,000-man force which is often referred to (and which includes women to whom noncombat duties are assigned) represents total mobilization. In a nation of only 2,600,000 people, including infants and the aged and infirm, nearly 10 per cent of the entire population on active duty results in a serious shortage of workers in the fields and the factories, in offices and stores, and in the professions and colleges. To Israel war means crippling disruption of social and economic life.

I have always had the greatest admiration for this gallant little country where men and women have struggled and continue to struggle to show what an energetic, dedicated people can do with what was, not so many years ago, an underdeveloped barren land. Some went there by choice, others by necessity, via the concentration camps of Europe and the prisons of North Africa. With different backgrounds and different skills they are well on the way to "making the desert bloom" and are more than anxious to "beat their swords into ploughshares"—if their neighbors would let them—in obedience to the dictates of their hearts and of their Scriptures to which we owe more than clichés. Instead, conditions since 1967 have obliged Israel to keep twice the usual number of reservists on active duty with resultant hardship, and to spend far too large a portion of her limited budget on defense and the purchase of obsolescent armaments. Having learned in 1967 that they could rely on no one to go to their defense, they have no alternative until a real and lasting peace is achieved—one which the Arabs must sincerely and freely obligate themselves to keep. Without it, they can neither afford to relax their defense nor be expected to surrender their territorial vantage points on which it depends to a great extent.

The President of the United States has recognized that this is so and has said that this country will not try to impose a peace. There is nothing to be gained by making Israel smaller, weaker, and more vulnerable. Territory is not the real issue in the Middle East today. Most of the boundaries in this area were determined, in any case, by either the British or the French. Boundary lines are not an insurmountable obstacle where there is friendship and cooperation between neighbors. If the demarcation lines between Israel and her Arab neighbors became a highway rather than a wall, the Arabs would gain considerably in technical assistance and trade and stand to win far more than they have lost.

I am convinced that these boundary lines can be swiftly determined and every other issue, including the vexed question of refugees, resolved if the parties meet in good faith and with honest intention. Neither the UN nor the Big Four have so far succeeded in setting the stage for such a meeting, mainly due to Arab insistence on Israeli withdrawal from occupied territories prior to discussion. As I said previously, we do not advocate such a course. America's best interest lies in strengthening Israel, not weakening her. That lesson was learned after the Suez-Sinai disaster when the administration pressured Israel into withdrawing from Suez, Sharm el Sheikh, Sinai, and Gaza. There were assurances that Israeli shipping would be allowed to navigate freely in the Straits of

Tiran and the Suez Canal; Nasser was not expected to return his forces to Gaza. But there were no guarantees. The result was the Six-Day War—ten years later.

At that time, in 1957, I was one of those who foresaw the danger, and I organized a group of forty Republican congressmen to try to alert the administration to it. If such a crisis were to recur today, I would not hesitate to act again. Apart from the moral and humanitarian side of the question—and who in his right mind could stand idly by while the Jewish people are once again threatened with genocide?—for the sake of world peace the Middle East must not be allowed to explode again. Too much is at stake.

While Russia's intentions remain unclear, she seems determined to assert her role as a Mediterranean power and is actively enlarging the naval and air base concessions already gained in Egypt. Intelligence sources report that Russian-made aircraft with Egyptian markings fly from Egyptian bases with Russian crews to carry out surveillance on the American Sixth Fleet in the Mediterranean, while Russian warships stand by in Egyptian ports. Eastern-bloc technicians and materiel have ensured that the Arab armed forces are better equipped today than ever before, despite the heavy 1967 losses.

It is obviously not in the interest of the United States for the Middle East to come into powerful and hostile hands. Nor is it in the interest of humanity to risk a third world war. *Crisis and Conscience in the Middle East* will make an important contribution to world peace if those who read and ponder it are led to take stock of their conscience—and to act upon it.

Crisis and conscience in the Middle East

1. The dimensions of crisis

The modern world has experienced no crisis more profound, more persistent, or more threatening than that which has beset the Middle East for more than two decades. It produced three wars in the twenty years preceding June 1967. The end is not yet in sight. Not a day has passed without the cruel legacy of war imposing its burden either directly or indirectly on the people of the area. One writer has suggested that the three wars were, in fact, just the hotter spots in one continuous war, the longest since Europe's Thirty Years' War of the seventeenth century.

On one side of the chasm of hostility stands Israel—small, embattled, alone, yet miraculously triumphant for the moment. On the other stands a coalition of Arab states, relatively large in population, backed in war by massive oil wealth (though the principal belligerents are not wealthy), supported by powerful states outside the Middle East, generously supplied with modern Soviet arms (as well as some of American origin), and smarting under a series of military setbacks at the hands of one small nation.

A great deal is at stake: the lives and property of Israel's 2.6 million people; the very right of Israel to exist as a free, sovereign state; the future of more than 600,000 Arab refugees; the welfare of 100 million inhabitants of the Arab lands and the lives of God only knows how many who may be jeopardized in the next round of general hostilities. One need not be a hawkish cold warrior to add, in the light of history and of the present Soviet involvement, the political independence of Egypt, Iraq, and Syria, and the existence of Jordan and its royal dynasty; the future of the whole region.

Persons with isolationist tendencies and minimal morals might be inclined to shrug off the Middle East crisis as something remote and of no concern to us. But the crisis won't stay at home. The confessed murderer of Senator Robert F. Kennedy was an immigrant from Palestine who cited Senator Kennedy's support of Israel as his motive. The American people were robbed of a dynamic and popular leader, and another profound tragedy was visited on an American family that has suffered much in the public service. The killer is reported to be a sort of folk hero among some supporters of the Arab guerrilla movement.

A direct military confrontation between the United States and the Soviet Union, possibly the opening round of World War III and the thermonuclear holocaust that all sane men dread, is one of the threats posed by the crisis. Neither the United States nor the Soviet Union has an immediate *vital* interest in the Middle East. Both are self-sufficient in oil, the chief economic prize of the region. But this does not mean that they do not have interests of varying import in the area. American oil companies have large investments there. Russia may have a desire to share the profits and to control the flow of Middle East petroleum to western Europe and eastern Asia, where it is needed. The Middle East is not without strategic importance, though that importance is not so great as it was when Suez was Britain's lifeline to India, or before the building of supertankers permitted the Cape route to eclipse the Suez Canal.

With her self-supporting naval forces, America is chiefly concerned that the Middle East not come into hands that are at once powerful and hostile. Russia's true intentions remain as enigmatic as Churchill found them. But the Soviets appear eager to enlarge the naval and air base concessions already gained in Egypt and to assert Russia's role as a Mediterranean power. American moral sense would be outraged if any administration failed to hinder the act of genocide that has been threatened against Israel. Meanwhile, China, no friend of either of the superpowers, has begun to dabble in the situation. A rational act of strategic self-interest, a mistake or miscalculation, an escalation of events that sucked in unwilling participants—any of these could turn the Middle East into an international tinderbox.

War is not the sole menace to international welfare that is posed by the crisis. The Congo crisis claimed the life of the greatest United Nations secretary general. The Middle East crisis threatens the life of the UN itself. Nowhere else has the peacekeeping organization failed so miserably to keep the peace. Nowhere else has it seemed more bent on discrediting itself in the eyes of thoughtful persons, whether by the antics of some of its members, the vote of a majority, or simply a failure of nerve.

These are all hard, practical considerations. But the Middle East crisis is more than a practical matter; it is a crisis and a burden to the conscience of mankind. I recognize that in saying this I am entering risky territory. As a historian I am aware that nearly every rogue and knave and predator in history has claimed the sanction of morality, if not the express will of God. It is no secret that specious claims to moral rectitude have exacerbated and prolonged many a human conflict. Nevertheless, I believe very strongly that there are identifiable and genuine moral issues germane to the Middle East crisis which cannot be overlooked by responsible persons.

1. Those who share with me the conviction that war and

killing are inherently evil need go no further to perceive a moral issue. One may recognize that violence sometimes seems unavoidable, that conscientious and thoughtful persons may consider war the lesser evil under the dispensation of history, without regarding it as morally desirable. War is much more likely to be eliminated in the Middle East and elsewhere by resolving its causes than by deploring war as such. Thus the fact of war constitutes a moral imperative to seek peaceful solutions.

2. The people of Israel have been threatened with genocide by their enemies. The evil of genocide is a nonnegotiable issue with civilized persons of every religious and philosophical persuasion.

3. The sovereign state of Israel has been threatened with extinction. The loss of sovereignty is surely a lesser evil than the loss of life, but for many of the victims it usually comes to the same thing. It would almost certainly mean extinction for Israel.

4. No Arab people has been threatened with genocide and no Arab state with politicide. Nevertheless, many hundreds of thousands of Palestinian Arab refugees have suffered deprivations that must be recognized as a burden to moral conscience *even if an intentional human agency*—Israeli or Arab *—cannot be assigned blame for every case or for a majority of cases.* As theologians have laid aside the intellectual arrogance that caused them to place the abstract problem of theodicy ahead of tangible human need, and as philosophers have inclined more universally toward humanism in ethics, it is increasingly recognized that suffering is bad, whoever or whatever causes it.

5. The overwhelming majority of the human victims of the crisis have been innocent persons who in no conscious way brought evil upon themselves. Even granting, for purposes of argument, that all the leaders of Zionism were rogues (a fabrication that appeals to some pro-Arab publicists) and/or that all Arab leaders were knaves (which would be a comforting rationalization for Israelis, though they don't use it), it would nevertheless remain true that the overwhelming majority of Jewish immigrants to Palestine went there in good

faith. They believed they had entered a country secured them by ancestral right, where they settled on land legally obtained. It would also remain true that misinformation, lack of information, decisions in which they played no part, and events beyond their comprehension have led Arab people to death and disaster.

The list could be extended, but this should suffice to make the point that persons capable of having moral concerns must include among them the Middle East crisis, once they have learned of it. Concern that stops with private guilt feelings or public hand-wringing hardly qualifies as moral. "Put your money where your mouth is," as we used to say in the Old Country. In other words, it is reasonable to ask that persons who are indignant over a problem involve themselves in promoting a solution. An immoral solution does not suffice for a moral problem, so just any solution will not do.

A great many people genuinely concerned about promoting a just and reasonable settlement to a problem are particularly valuable when the problem has achieved crisis proportions. Crisis tends to polarize opinion and freeze it into dogmatism. Clearly the Middle East crisis has done this, and not only in the region itself. There are overly polite circles in which the subject simply isn't mentioned. But polarized people are in a state of estrangement, on a collision course, like two aircraft in a fog with no radar or radio. Unpolarized people may serve the function of defusing the crisis, of draining off the charge, so to speak. They may act as buffers, as mediums of communication, as sources of constructive initiative. To be unpolarized is not to be devoid of convictions or opinions, but to remain open, flexible, and committed to nonviolent resolution. To be sure, a crisis may become so exacerbated that a person with any convictions worth mentioning must consult his best judgment (fallible though it be) and cast his lot as it dictates. This is precisely what rational men want to avoid. Thus the possibility that this may happen gives an added note of urgency to the quest for settlement.

This extended essay is offered in the hope that it may encourage more people to join the quest for a humane resolution of the Middle East crisis. The essay has a point of view, and I see no purpose in trying to conceal the fact behind a façade of academic neutrality. I am not interested in scoring superficial debate points, nor do I propose to reciprocate the vituperation my views have drawn from persons whose words and manners are in any case more interesting to the psychopathologist than to the historian. If a reader rejects all I say but becomes or remains devoted to a peaceful and equitable solution of the conflict between Israel and the Arab states, I shall have no complaint.

I believe the people of Israel, like every people, have the right to live free from the threat of genocide. I believe the state of Israel stands on viable foundations and has the same right to sovereign existence as any other nation. (These two statements would be greeted with amazement if the name of any other nation were substituted for Israel. Cannot these rights be taken for granted?) I believe the military actions Israel has taken in her own defense have been justified by the threats and belligerent actions directed against her, though I would not argue that every single one was wise. Only time will permit a judgment concerning Israel's conquests in the Six-Day War of June 1967.

If Israel casts aside the prospect of a genuine settlement in order to appropriate these lands in a greedy manner, the action will be culpable. If she liquidates them in the cause of peace, the action will constitute an unusual gesture of generosity in the history of statecraft. What Israel is *able* to do will be governed by the actions of her neighbors and other states severally and in concert, for the Middle East crisis is far from a one-nation show.

This leads to a final statement of belief. The single greatest barrier to settlement in the Middle East is the truculence and obstinacy of the dominant faction among the leaders of the Arab belligerents. I think I understand to a great extent why they act as they do, but to understand and to approve are —contrary to a popular misconception—not quite the same thing.

I have not held these views lightly or without subjecting them to critical evaluation in the face of available evidence.

23. The dimensions of crisis

Recently I devoted the major part of a sabbatical leave to the study of the Middle East and its history, including the present conflict. Not all of those I encountered shared my views. Among those who disagreed, I confess a particular debt to those American and Arab scholars whose compassionate and thoughtful manner have led those who would tread the path of reason to reflect much more searchingly than all the anti-Zionist crusaders put together.

Those who are fond of labels may wish to hang the "pro-Israel" tag on this work. I accept the designation, so long as one does not draw the unwarranted implication that what-ever is pro-Israel is also anti-Arab. In the course of this dis-cussion I shall be obliged to pass criticism on the actions of our British friends, though I doubt that will erase my well-founded reputation as an Anglophile. I shall also be making blunt statements about malfunctions of the United Nations, yet I know I shall continue to send UNICEF cards at Christ-mastime, and I expect to go on defending the UN against radicals of the left and right. By the same token, I do not reject my Arab or pro-Arab friends. I do not negate the positive contributions President Nasser and other Arab lead-ers have made to the welfare of their own people, though I believe their wrongheadedness about Israel has reduced their potential for constructive action. I do not withhold humane concern from the Arab peoples.

Indeed, I would argue that my position is pro-Arab in the most significant sense. It seeks for both sides a just and hon-orable settlement, which is the only kind that can last and promise a bright future for Arab or Jew. It seeks recompense for the Arab refugees beyond what most courts of equity would allow. It discourages the Arab nations from actions they would have to be ashamed of on reflection after the fact, if not before. It aims at a peace that would certainly benefit the Arabs as much as the Israelis in the short run and even more in the long run. It takes the Arabs much more seriously as human beings than some of their patronizing Western syco-phants are wont to do. It demands no concessions of Arab honor—only acceptance of Mr. Churchill's axiom, "Jaw, jaw, jaw is better than war, war, war." As a matter of fact, I wonder

24. The dimensions of crisis

if I have not been more generous to the Arab side—and consequently less fair to Israel—than events may justify. As I prepared the final revisions of this book, the sad news of the fire that gutted part of the Al Aksa Mosque in the Haram es Sharif compound of old Jerusalem was current. The contrast between Arab and Israeli reaction to this unfortunate loss to the faithful of Islam and to all patrons of antiquity was glaring. Israel's prime minister, Mrs. Golda Meir, issued a touching statement of sympathy, and Israel's government launched a searching investigation. A foreigner, neither Jew nor Arab but a Western Christian, was arrested by Israeli police and confessed to arson. Meanwhile, Arab mobs were roused to demonstrate in Jerusalem and Nablus. Israeli security troops, stoned by mobs, fired over the heads of their assailants. President Nasser declared that the fire convinced him that force must be used against Israel. Some Arab quarters agitated for holy war and sought to involve the whole Moslem world.

A Moslem summit conference was held in Rabat, Morocco, to discuss the incident. Perhaps the most significant document to come before it was a fraternal appeal from Pope Paul VI, which reads, in part: "The appeal to religious sentiment, far from maintaining division, should take form as a principle of union that would permit the surmounting of both political and military antagonisms and lead toward understanding and peace" (Associated Press wire story of September 24, 1969).

One begins to suspect that if an Arab suffered malnutrition during the Ramadan fast, that too would be charged against Israel. But if one is to err, let it be on the side of generosity. Thus do Judaism, Islam, and Christianity teach. Thus one is supposed to approach the ways of peace.

2. The rise of Zionism

The forces of modern history might have ensured that the Middle East would be a troubled region, even without the rebirth of Israel. But the Middle East crisis today is quite incomprehensible apart from the quest for a restored Jewish homeland in Palestine—the quest known as Zionism.

Zionism as a well-organized and effective public movement is a relatively modern phenomenon. But Zionism as such has ancient and deep roots. It is as old as the dispersion of the Israelite tribes from their landholdings, one of the consequences of the wars of antiquity. The dispersion really began with the fall and partial exile of the northern Israelite kingdom under the lash of Assyria in the late eighth century B.C. It was accelerated by the successive Babylonian conquests and deportations in the lands of Benjamin and Judah from 597 down into the 580s B.C. The Babylonian exile produced the first active Zionist movement, the return of Jewish exiles from Babylon to Jerusalem after more tolerant Persia supplanted Babylon as the great Middle Eastern empire. The returnees combined with the people who had been left at home to reconstitute the social and religious life of Israel and to rebuild the ruined temple on Zion, the sacred mountain of Jerusalem. Three and a half centuries would pass before the Jewish people again would breathe free air on their own soil, but the foundations had been secured.

A short-lived era of political independence and the restoration of a territory approximating the traditional Israelite kingdom was achieved by the Jews under Maccabean leadership in the second pre-Christian century. The rising power of Rome, however, had engulfed Israel before the dawn of the Christian era. The Jews' passion for freedom and communal integrity ill prepared them to be subservient recipients of Roman imperialism's checkered blessings. Israel was almost alone among ancient peoples in risking two wars for independence against Rome. The courses of both wars (67–72 A.D., 132–135 A.D.) were similar. Jewish heroism and military prowess gained initial victories, but Rome had the means to drown the insurgents in a sea of blood and matériel, and she was no more tolerant of independent-minded colonials than more modern tyrants. Both revolts ended with terrible carnage as the relentless Roman army ground its way to victory over outnumbered and ill-equipped rebels. Jewish prisoners were slaughtered in the arena to entertain Romans and their toadies. Leaders were executed by crucifixion and other forms of torture. Multitudes were sold into slavery.

Religious teachers, such as Jesus and most of the leading Pharisees, had opposed war in general and warned of the consequences of war with Rome. The direst prophecies were realized. Jews were subjected to repressive laws and banned from Jerusalem, while a Roman town with pagan temples was constructed upon the ruins of the Holy City. The Jewish commonwealth was dead for the next eighteen hundred years.

27. The rise of Zionism

The Jews were a people without a country, without a government, without a trustworthy physical defense. Even the name of their homeland was changed. Formerly known as "the Land of Israel" or "the Land of Judah," or called in ancient inscriptions by one of the names of the reigning Israelite king, it now became Palestine by Roman convention to all but the faithful of Israel.

These disasters nevertheless did not extinguish Jewish love and longing for the homeland, nor did they terminate Jewish residence in Palestine. As a result of the centuries of dispersion, at the beginning of the Christian era there were more Jews living outside Judah and Galilee than within them. But residents of the dispersion continued to regard Israel as the center of their religious life, despite flourishing centers of Jewish scholarship and spirituality in Babylon, Alexandria, and elsewhere. Brilliant rabbinic scholars of the dispersion (such as St. Paul) returned to the Holy Land in quest of fulfillment. The pious bent every effort to make a pilgrimage to Jerusalem at the great festivals. A great rabbinic academy persisted after the disasters, first at Jabneh (Jamnia) and later at Tiberias in Galilee. The lot of Jews in their homeland and elsewhere was made no easier by the misguided zeal of the Christian emperors of Rome, from Constantine onward. Jews in the Holy Land and other eastern provinces found some relief after the Moslem conquest. The Koran accords Christianity and Judaism an honorable status as "religions of the book," albeit a status clearly subordinate to Islam's. Thus Jews remained second-class citizens in their homeland.

The Holy Land remained a magnet for pious Jews. Beset by persecution here, expulsion there, some undertook the arduous journey to Zion, the center of their longing. During the Middle Ages Jewish communities flourished at Safad, the great center of mystical piety in Galilee, at Tiberias, at Jerusalem, and at Hebron beside the traditional tomb of the patriarchs. The spirit of what can only be called medieval Zionism is aptly caught in the *Zion Ode* of the scholar-poet Judah ha-Levi, who perished on a pilgrimage to Jerusalem.

> Have we any heritage save the sanctuaries of God?
> Thus how should we forget His Holy Mount?
> Have we either in the east or in the west
> A place of hope wherein we may trust,
> Except in that land which is full of gates,
> Toward which the gates of Heaven are open . . .?
> Unto us, yea, and unto our children hath He
>   assigned her. . . .*

Those with lesser poetic gifts than Judah were reminded of their bond with the Holy Land by the words spoken each year over the Passover meal: "Next year in Jerusalem!"

The false messianic movements of the seventeenth and eighteenth centuries raised and then dashed Jewish hopes for a restored Israel, as did the on-again-off-again prospect that the Turkish sultanate would reestablish the Jewish state as a matter of imperial policy. It was only toward the mid-nineteenth century that a concerted movement to mount organized Jewish resettlement in the Holy Land developed in Europe. This modern Zionist movement was fired from a number of sources, among them a revival of Jewish learning and letters, the romanticism of the era, the wide stirrings of nationalism, and successive persecutions of Jews in eastern Europe. Historians frequently identify the First Zionist Congress (Basel, 1897) as the point of serious beginning. Actually, the Congress marked the reorganization and revitalization of a movement already well along the way. Such British philanthropists as Sir Moses Montefiore, Lawrence Oliphant, and the Earl of Shaftesbury were underwriting the efforts of Jewish settlers in the Holy Land as early as the 1850s. (One of the windmills Sir Moses built to improve Jerusalem's water supply still stands near the King David Hotel. The coach in which he toured the struggling Jewish settlements is displayed nearby.) Baron Edmond de Rothschild, of the great French banking house, took a strong interest in the Palestinian settlements from 1883 onward.

The Dreyfus Affair in France provided a powerful impetus

*Lines 28–32, 37. See *Kuzari*, bk. 2, secs. 9–24, for Judah's discursive treatment of the same theme.

Early Jewish pioneers of the 1880's from Poland and Russia.

for Zionist action in Europe. An antidemocratic clique framed young Captain Alfred Dreyfus (who happened to be Jewish) on a charge of passing military secrets to Germany. Apparently they hoped to use Dreyfus as a lever to pry loose an avalanche of anti-Semitic hatred that could be channeled to undermine the French Republic. The documents used to convict Dreyfus were proven forgeries, so the cabal fabricated new evidence. Dreyfus was condemned to Devil's Island at his first trial in 1894, and it was 1906 before he was cleared. Meanwhile there had been a massive outpouring of anti-Semitic passion, and the tentacles of fraud were traced to the higher ranks of army, government, and church. The honor of France was thoroughly sullied.

France prided herself on being the most enlightened nation in the world. The bigotry revealed in the course of the Dreyfus Affair and the fact that the perpetrators went unpunished and smug in their self-righteousness while the victims were uncompensated generated a shock through the civilized world. If Jews were not safe in the self-styled mecca of enlightenment, where could they be safe?

30. The rise of Zionism

A young Austrian Jewish writer, Theodor Herzl, was among the journalists covering the Dreyfus trial. What he observed changed him from a man indifferent to his heritage into the driving personal force of the Zionist movement. Herzl's book *Der Judenstaat (The Jewish State)* became a platform for Zionism. His diaries record the private reflections of a man bent on swaying history. Herzl became, as it were, the patron saint of Zionism. He dared to dream of a revived Israel on its native soil within fifty years of the First Zionist Congress. He proved himself to be an able soothsayer, in no small part because of his own energetic labors.

The Holy Land was ruled by the Ottoman Turkish Empire as a part of its province of Southern Syria at the end of the nineteenth century and the beginning of the twentieth. The dominant population group was nominally Arabic, divided among Moslems and various Eastern Christian persuasions. The land itself was in a sorry state. The wars of antiquity had contributed to deforestation and the collapse of intensive agricultural works. Arabic cultural vitality had been in decline for centuries. Peasant agricultural practices had gone through unfortunate changes. The Oriental tradition of maladministration was not absent. Various Western powers, principally Britain, France, Germany, and Russia, were involved in Palestine for reasons of their own. In theory they were merely looking out for the religious interests of various Christian denominations. In fact they were exercising concessions granted by the Ottomans in return for military favors. Thus the Zionist leaders not only had to concern themselves with negotiations with the Ottoman government, always delicate business at best, but also had to be aware of shifts of wind blowing from the chancelleries of Europe.

Jewish and Gentile philanthropy financed the purchase of land from Arab landholders by Zionist organizations and the establishment of Jewish settlers on it. The land the owners were willing to sell was often in deplorable condition—either swamp or desert. But in spite of this the Jewish settlers turned their holdings into garden spots. Later, under the British mandate, the Zionists also obtained long-term leases on land that Ottoman records showed to be government property.

Theodor Herzl, the father of modern political Zionism, on his way to Palestine in 1898.

World War I changed the face of the Middle East. While modern Turkey rose miraculously from the shambles of the Ottoman Empire, Franco-British diplomacy was shaping the Arab segments of the former Ottoman territories into protectorates and, they hoped, tractable Arab principalities. Palestine, formerly an administrative part of Syria, was carved off by the British, a League of Nations mandate having legitimated the surgery. Iraq and the newly created state of Transjordan were placed in the British sphere of influence. French supremacy was established in Syria and Lebanon. European colonialism had its last grand fling. Some Arabic tribes had fought on the Allied side against the Austro-German-Ottoman axis and hoped freedom would be their reward. They discovered that Whitehall and the Quai d'Orsay still considered them "lesser breeds without the law," in need of European tutelage.

32. The rise of Zionism

During the war Britain had issued the famous Balfour Declaration, which promised a Jewish national home in Palestine while protecting the full rights of the indigenous population. The declaration clashed somewhat with assurances of lesser diplomatic stature which Britain had earlier given Arab leaders. As a result, different interpretations of British intentions were apparently communicated to Zionists and Arabs. Indeed, the practice of interpreting British policy differently to the Zionists and to the Arabs seems to have become standard procedure. All parties subsequently suffered on this account.

Britain's League of Nations mandate included the responsibility of executing the terms of the Balfour Declaration, with the endorsement of prominent Arab leaders. But Britain had hardly made the promise of a Jewish homeland before she began to renege on it. Arab dislike of Zionism grew, and Arab counters were weighing more heavily in the diplomatic balances. The years between the two world wars were difficult for Zionism. Jewish migration to Palestine was limited by the British in deference to Arab pressure. Even the limited quotas were not filled in some years, and money was short. After Hitler began his persecutions in Germany, however, the quotas were never adequate to meet the demand. Zionists were obliged to resort to clandestine immigration simply to rescue lives from the Nazis. Jewish land purchases were restricted by the British in further accommodation to Arab wishes.

The Arabs of Palestine had on balance never welcomed the new Jewish settlers. Modern research suggests that Arab-Jewish relations were never quite so good in the period before the large-scale modern immigration as popular tradition would have it. Even in the mid-nineteenth century, "Jew" seems to have been a term of contempt among Palestinian Arabs. The Moslem record on the treatment of Jews prior to 1948 looks good largely by comparison with Christendom's sorry record of anti-Semitic persecution. Nevertheless, the various Moslem governments that had controlled the Holy Land from the early Middle Ages recognized the right of Jews to come as permanent residents. (This right was not accorded Western Christians in a region where "Crusader" remains a bad word.)

33. The rise of Zionism

The Zionist migrants were a different sort of Jew from the Orthodox Oriental pietists familiar to Arab experience. These newcomers did not know their place as a minority in an Arab Moslem region. Nor were they about to let their place be defined by relics of seventh-century Arab imperialism. Further, the Zionist land purchases had the effect in some instances of displacing former Arab tenants and day laborers. The Jewish settlers wanted to be farmers, not absentee landlords. Their agriculture was organized on highly functional, albeit utopian, lines. The *kibbutzim* (communal farms) had no need for hired labor. The utopian idealism of the Zionist pioneers thus innocently alienated some of their neighbors. The Jewish settlements did not threaten to overpopulate the country, as some allege, nor did the Arab population increase out of hand. There was and still is open land in Palestine. The state of Israel today supports a population larger than the total population of Palestine in the first quarter of this century on less land than the area of the British mandate. It would do so with a surplus economy were it not obliged to carry a crushing burden of defense expenditures. Actually, the Zionist program increased the available land by reclaiming marginal or totally unproductive areas and by revivifying the Negev, dormant since ancient times. The problem is not land but water. Irrigation has extended agricultural and residential possibilities in both Israel and Jordan, and a great deal more could be accomplished with existing resources under conditions of peaceful cooperation, even without application of the new desalinization technology, which could eliminate both thirst and land hunger in the region for centuries to come.

Economic life in Palestine had been on the upswing since Western interest was renewed in the eighteenth and especially the nineteenth centuries. Western interest also led to improvements in public health, medical care, and education. These trends were accelerated by the growing Jewish settlement. Palestinian Arabs were substantial beneficiaries of such developments. The Arab population grew during those years, both by natural increase and by immigration (much of it unregistered). But Arab achievements were inevitably outstripped by those of the better educated and technologically more accomplished Jewish migrants. Many Arabs were frightened by the prospect that they might become the minority in a land where they had formerly been the majority. Worse, they feared that they might find themselves in a land where Jews held viable political power—in short, a world turned upside down. Lastly, the Zionists were organized. They had to organize in order to achieve the formidable tasks of migration, settlement, education, health care, and construction which they had undertaken. The Jewish Agency was recognized by the Mandate authorities as representative of Palestinian Jewry. The Arabs were badly disorganized, and when they did try to join together to form counterpart organizations (such as the Arab Higher Committee), they found their establishments less adaptive and resourceful than those of the Jews.

Arab dislike, fear, and frustration began to express itself in growing acts of violence against Jews through the 1920s and 1930s. Many of the Palestinian Jews were religious pacifists who considered it better to die at the hands of persecutors than to strike in self-defense. British police protection was less than even-handed from a Jewish viewpoint. The British seemed more enthusiastic about confiscating arms held by Jews than those held by Arabs. An underground Jewish self-defense organization was developed to prevent such outrages as the massacres at Hebron and elsewhere in 1929. Haganah, the defense organization, was the seed of the Jewish Brigade, which fought valiantly on the Allied side in World War II (while the Arab mufti of Jerusalem consorted with Hitler), and of the Army of Israel.

During these years too many Palestinian Arabs fell into an unfortunate but highly predictable pattern of response to every encounter with Zionism: total intransigence, followed by resort to violence, followed by an appeal to outside agencies to bail them out when the violent solution misfired. A large segment of the Arab world outside Palestine apparently has since become caught in this unproductive pattern, and support from outsiders has encouraged the more truculent to believe that they can have their *deus ex machina*, whatever they may do. One must hope that sensitive Arab leadership will recognize the sterility of this response pattern and will assert itself to direct the considerable talents and energies of the Arab peoples toward a more humane and creative means of resolving their differences with their Jewish neighbors. Sadly, this did not happen in the early formative years of the encounter.

Jewish people around the world were themselves not universally enthusiastic about Zionism. The native Oriental Jews of Palestine initially looked with some suspicion on immigrants who belonged to a different liturgical tradition and who evinced unfamiliar customs. The most conservative Orthodox expected God to restore Israel miraculously in the days of the Messiah, and lodged little confidence in a secular program. The most liberal Jews viewed Zionism as a step backward from their goal of increasing accommodation to optimistic Western humanism. Others, smugly content with their own lot, were simply indifferent to the struggle of their brethren far away.

The horror of the Nazi holocaust served to galvanize to the Zionist cause not only an overwhelming majority of world Jewry, but humanitarians of every community and persuasion as well. If the Dreyfus Affair was a shock, Hitler's "final solution of the Jewish problem" was a cataclysm of cosmic proportions. Nineteenth-century France may have prided herself on her enlightenment; twentieth-century Germany was the most literate, best educated nation in the world. As a matter of empirical fact, Germany was the one nation—possibly excepting the United States—in which Jews had become most fully an integrated and productive part of national life. If it could happen in Germany, it could happen anywhere. And it had happened in Germany. Not just a pogrom or series of pogroms, not just a massacre or series of massacres, but a systematic scheme of genocide that extinguished six million Jewish lives within Hitler's dominion. It has been properly pointed out that Jews were not Hitler's only victims. No one has ever said they were. They were simply his explicit target and his principal victims. More than one-third of the world Jewish population was annihilated by the Nazis. No other people can make that statement.

The enormity of the Hitlerite crime was not the only factor promoting the Zionist cause. The callous response of the international community to the fate of Hitler's victims was deplorable. Early international action might have stayed the Nazi death machine in its tracks, but none was evident. The death camps were mere "Zionist propaganda." The civilized Germans wouldn't—couldn't—do such a thing. Countless lives could have been saved had the free nations opened their door to Jewish refugees. A few doors were opened a crack, mostly for physicians, scientists, and scholars of international repute, though not always even for them. British expediency kept the lid on immigration to the refuge of Palestine. Only a few Latin American countries have a record they may be proud of from those sad days.

When the Allied armies swept across Europe, the world saw a truth that it has not even yet been willing to accept fully. But even in the partial light of truth it was abundantly clear to all who had eyes to see that Jews, like everybody else, had a right to a national home, a place where they might be free from oppression and persecution, a place where they might form their own destiny, a place where they might develop their own humane heritage without apology. The place had to be Palestine. Zionism had steadfastly refused to become party to European colonialism and declined tempting offers of rich lands in Africa which were put forth as alternatives to Palestine. The Jewish people had been scattered from their ancestral homeland by war, deprivation, and other circumstances of history. But they had never renounced their claim to it. Quite the contrary: they proclaimed their loyalty to it across the centuries of dispersion. But for a few interludes of Roman and Byzantine repression, their right to return to Palestine had always been recognized.

Now they were coming back. Though they came in peace, the second Jewish return from exile would not be peaceful. It would fuel the longest marathon crisis of the twentieth century.

3. The rebirth of Israel

World War II proved a catalyst for nationalist and anti-colonial sentiment throughout the world. The Arabic peoples nursed legitimate grievances against the European powers for the shabby treatment accorded them after World War I. Arab disunity paved the way for European exploitation. But however justified, the action of Western powers merited the contempt of Arab nationalism, as the bad faith that followed the promulgation of the Balfour Declaration merited that of Jewish nationalism in its Zionist form.

The conclusion of World War II found the powers of western Europe prostrate. Britain, badly drained, faced the reluctant necessity of liquidating her empire, and Mr. Churchill's brave words to the contrary, a Tory victory in the postwar elections would not have altered the case. Having suffered tremendously and lacking the means to apply her massive land forces so far from home, Russia was obliged to content herself with a satellite empire in eastern Europe (American insistence dislodged Russian troops from the wartime supply line through Iran). The United States emerged as the only viable world power at the conclusion of hostilities and for a decade thereafter. But Americans lacked the appetite for old-fashioned imperialism. The way was open for Arab and other nationalisms to be asserted.

Jewish nationalism encountered the largest number of difficulties. The Zionist dream, or even its first approximation, seemed thwarted, despite great worldwide popular support. The nations' governments seemed no more eager to salvage the survivors of Hitler's terror than they had been to help them and their millions of now dead compatriots while the ovens still smoked. Zionism stood ready to shoulder the arduous burden of assimilating the refugees into the Jewish community of Palestine. Britain stood in the way. Bowing to Arab wishes, the British kept the lid on Jewish immigration clamped tight. Ravaged survivors of Nazism rusticated in European "displaced persons" camps. Many attempted clandestine entry to the Promised Land. Those apprehended by mandate authorities were stored behind barbed wire once again.

The mandate rested heavily on British will and resources, depleted by a recent struggle for survival. The problems it posed seemed insoluble. Zionists insisted that the promise of a Jewish national home in Palestine be kept. Arab nationalists were adamantly opposed. The climate of international opinion as expressed in the fledgling United Nations failed to support Britain's generally pro-Arab policy. Britain brought the problem to the UN in exhaustion and frustration. The United Nations Special Committee on Palestine (UNSCOP) was created in 1947 to investigate and report recommendations to the General Assembly.

No single Zionist plan for realizing the Jewish national home existed. The great majority probably favored the inclusion of all cis-Jordan Palestine in a Jewish state. Some extremists wanted a Jewish state that would include Trans-

The British deny the refugee-laden Exodus *permission to dock in Palestine, forcing her passengers to return to Germany.*

jordan as well. Such influential figures as the philosopher Martin Buber (the man who created the "I-thou" concept), and Judah Magnes, founding president of the Hebrew University, advocated the creation of a binational or, more accurately, a bicultural state in which Jews and Arabs would share a common national life.

A British royal commission had proposed the partition of Palestine into Jewish and Arab states as early as 1937. Others entertained the notion of a scheme of federated Jewish and Arab cantons in Palestine on something like the Swiss model.

The unfortunate Arab reaction cycle of intransigence, violence, and appeal for help began to assert itself again. Arab leaders made it plain they would settle for a solution only on their own terms. The Arab Higher Committee, dominated by the anti-Jewish, pro-Nazi mufti, recognized by the British as the official voice of Palestinian Arabs, proposed the deportation of all "illegal" Jewish immigrants. Apparently the Higher Committee was to determine which immigrants were legal and which illegal. All of Palestine would become an Arab state. Such a solution would leave the Palestinian Jews in the same precarious position Jewry had suffered for two thousand years, if not worse. The subsequent behavior of some Arab states leaves it unclear as to what form an Arab Palestine might have taken. More aggressive outsiders might have simply carved it into pieces for themselves.

UNSCOP did not begin its investigation with a predetermined solution in mind. Much of its work was carried out on the ground in Palestine. Various proposals were received from Zionist representatives who indicated that they would accept partition as an alternative. The Arab Higher Committee refused to testify. The British Mandate administration insisted on the privilege of secret testimony. The Arab League states presented their views at a special UNSCOP session in Lebanon. A subcommittee flew to Amman to hear Jordanian opinions. Perhaps the most depressing discovery by UNSCOP beyond the hostile complexity of the situation was Britain's poor stewardship of her League mandate. Not only had the responsibility to execute the Balfour Declaration been bankrupted, but provisions for the welfare of the Arab population were far below reasonable expectations. And in its latter days, the mandate administration seemed bent on proving it could out-Nazi the Gestapo. Ad hoc legislation by executive fiat, arbitrary judicial behavior, and unbridled police activity were recounted to UNSCOP, smudging the proud British claim to symbolize the rule of law.

The *Exodus 1947* incident (the real and tragic *Exodus*, not the fictional and triumphant one) coincided with the UNSCOP investigation. A small, fragile, unarmed steamer loaded with refugees from the Nazi holocaust escaped Europe despite the machinations of British power politics. British intelligence and diplomatic services sought to obstruct its trying journey across the Mediterranean while an escort of six British warships (including the famous cruiser *Ajax*) harassed its course. The climax came off Haifa when British warships rammed and boarded the *Exodus* in international waters. The crew and refugees defended themselves with fists, unpeeled potatoes, and food cans against British clubs, bullets, and tear gas. It was a futile defense. The survivors were deported—to Germany.

One man's terrorist is another man's heroic freedom fighter. But terrorist activity was a fact of daily life in Palestine. The Western press gave a much larger play to the activities of the Jewish extremist organizations Irgun Zvai Leumi (National Military Organization) and the Fighters for the Freedom of Israel (also known as the Stern Gang) than to the deeds of Arab groups. Perhaps Western journalists recognized terrorism to be out of harmony with the Jewish spirit and Zionism's lofty ideals. Thus, even though Irgun and the Sternists may have helped persuade the British to get out, their works were no help to Zionism's reputation in the West. A great deal was made of the fact that Jews would not betray the extremists. It was much less noticed that the overwhelming majority of Jews would have no part of terrorism. In fact, Haganah assumed the task of thwarting terrorist plots on its own, including a plan to blow up the British military headquarters in Tel Aviv. Irgun's most spectacular exploits were the bombing of a wing of the King David Hotel that was being used as British military quarters, and a raid on Acre Prison which freed both Jewish and Arab political prisoners. Anti-Jewish terrorists were quite active themselves. The actions of such persons reached a climax in early 1948, when men in British uniforms took a convoy of trucks loaded with explosives to Ben Yehudah Street in Jewish Jerusalem and there detonated the load. Violent death came to 175 Jewish civilians. Injury and property damage were extensive.

The states of intracommunal hostility and Arab obduracy served to convince unscop that partition was not only the most desirable but the only possible solution to the Palestine problem. But how could an equitable partition be drawn for a small country with the illogical geography of Palestine? In the concluding years of the mandate the Jewish population in Palestine stood at about 600,000, the Arab population at over a million. By far the greater amount of titled land belonged to Arabs, a circumstance rendered more glaring by the British embargo on Jewish land purchases. The scattered nature of Jewish holdings complicated matters further. An exclusively Jewish and an exclusively Arab state would necessitate considerable relocation. Thus the developing UN plan envisioned a Jewish state with a sizable Arab minority and an Arab state with a small Jewish minority. The Jewish state would include eastern Galilee, a strip of the coastal plain from a point above Haifa to a point between Tel Aviv and Gaza (excluding Jaffa), and most of the Negev. The Arab state would consist of western Galilee to the sea at Acre, the highlands of Samaria and Judah, an enclave around Jaffa, the Gaza Strip, and a section of the western Negev. A small territory encompassing Jerusalem and Bethlehem would enjoy neutral status under UN trusteeship. An economic union of the two states was projected.

Arab rejection of partition in principle was already a matter of record. The UN plan was further attacked in Arab quarters on the ground that it gave the best land to the Jewish state. Ironically, the plan gave the Arab state the historic Israelite heartland and placed two of Judaism's holiest sites, Jerusalem and Hebron, under other administration.

The UN General Assembly set up a special ad hoc committee on Palestine to deal with the UNSCOP report and various counterproposals in the autumn of 1947. The ad hoc committee adopted a procedure that ensured that diametrically opposed plans, one for a unitary Palestinian state and one a revision of the UNSCOP partition plan, would come to the Assembly. Alternatives such as the proposal of a small UNSCOP minority to revive the notion of federated cantons had little chance for consideration. Sentiment in the Assembly favored partition, though surely another scheme that promised to conciliate Jewish and Arab differences would have received a sympathetic hearing. The Arab bloc sought and nearly got

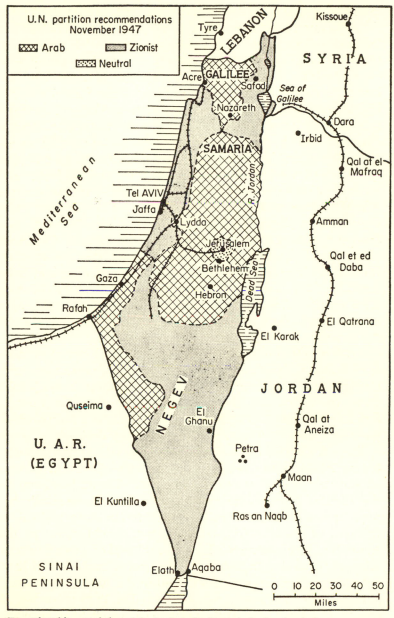

U.N. partition recommendations
November 1947

▨ Arab   ▨ Zionist
▨ Neutral

Tyre

LEBANON

Kissoue

S Y R I A

Acre   GALILEE

Safad

Nazareth

*Sea of
Galilee*

Dara

Irbid

Qal at el
Mafraq

SAMARIA

R. Jordan

*Mediterranean
Sea*

Tel AVIV

Jaffa

Lydda

Amman

Jerusalem

Qal et ed
Daba

Bethlehem

Dead Sea

Gaza

Hebron

Rafah

El Qatrana

El Karak

J O R D A N

NEGEV

Quseima

El
Ghanu

Qal at
Aneiza

U. A. R.
(E G Y P T)

Petra

Maan

El Kuntilla

Ras an Naqb

S I N A I
P E N I N S U L A

Elath   Aqaba

0   10 20 30 40 50

Miles

(Reproduced by permission of the *Institute for Strategic Studies*, London) passage of a resolution to request a World Court ruling on the competence of the UN to enact partition. This would have delayed partition, but the inheritance of League credentials by the UN, the treaties that ended World War I, and the fact that no Palestinian sovereignty had existed since the fall of the Second Jewish Commonwealth made it likely that the court would have upheld UN competence.

Events moved toward a climax in the latter part of November 1947. Britain made known her wish that the mandate be terminated as soon as possible. Alarmed by the support for partition in the Assembly, Arab delegations suddenly revived the federation plan. Had Arab support for this alternative been strong and forthcoming earlier in the game, it might have carried the day. Such a plan, properly drawn, was probably the best hope for a peaceful and mutually beneficial solution to the Palestine problem. It wasn't a favorite with the majority of Zionist leaders, but they were practical people who were capable of recognizing that one's preferred solution was not necessarily the most viable solution. After all, partition was not initially Zionism's first choice. Coming as late as it did, however, the Arab move—even if it was sincere—was bound to look like a delaying tactic. Another Arab-supported move to adjourn the Assembly until January 15, 1948, was indeed a delaying tactic. Partition had gained too much momentum. Even those who suspected that it was less than an ideal solution embraced it as superior to no solution at all. On November 29, 1947, the United Nations General Assembly voted 33 to 13, with 10 abstentions, to adopt the ad hoc committee's partition plan. An interesting aspect of the action in the light of more recent history was Russia's enthusiastic support of partition. For once the Soviet Union and the United States voted the same way on a controversial issue.

The United Nations found itself in the uncomfortable position of having made a decision that it lacked the will really to enforce, even if it could muster the means. Britain had announced she would play no part in executing a decision that was not acceptable to both sides, and partition was anathema to the Arabs. The burgeoning cold war made it un-

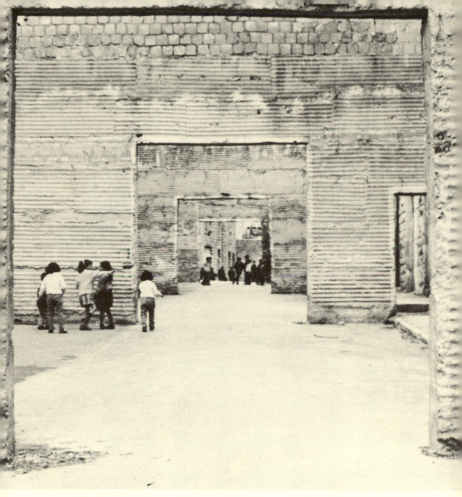

Jerusalem divided, from 1948 to 1967. A series of walls
which separate East and West Jerusalem.

likely that either the United States or the USSR would support the creation of a UN force in which the other might
have overbalancing influence. The United Nations was left
with the force of international public opinion and the power
of moral suasion on its side, both notoriously ineffective
against firearms. Indeed, some governments, including the
United States as represented by the State Department, appeared ready to hedge on their votes for partition. To all
intents and purposes, the Jews of Palestine were left to make
their way in a hostile land—not a new experience for Jews.

46. The rebirth of Israel

Britain announced that its mandate would be terminated on May 15, 1948, but would not admit UN supervisory personnel to Palestine before May 1. Arab leadership had long trumpeted its determination to prevent partition by force and to make war on the UN if it attempted to enforce its decision. Trained "volunteers" from various Arab states joined Palestinian Arab war parties as the tempo of Arab-Jewish hostilities quickened. British forces began a staged withdrawal timed to be completed with the end of the mandate.

The state of Israel was proclaimed in a solemn assembly at the Municipal Museum at Tel Aviv on May 14, 1948. President Harry S. Truman extended almost immediate United States diplomatic recognition in one of those courageous acts for which he was famous. Russian recognition followed shortly. So did foreign invaders. Troops of Egypt, Jordan, Syria, Iraq, and Lebanon invaded Israel on May 15, on the heels of the withdrawing British. Soon they were joined by contingents from Saudi Arabia and Yemen.

The new nation of Israel was obliged to fight for her life against considerable odds and with little overt external support. Twenty-four hundred private volunteers from all over the world rallied to Israel's banner. They were both Jews and non-Jews. Badly needed equipment had to be acquired the hard way. The British had sought with some success to keep Palestinian Jews disarmed.

The new Jewish section of West Jerusalem was besieged early in the hostilities. Arabs held the pumping station at Latrun and cut the water supply. Arab forces invested the most precarious section of the road from Tel Aviv to Jerusalem. Many brave Israeli drivers perished attempting to run a gantlet of fire through the mountains with supplies for Jerusalem. The shattered hulks of their vehicles still stand in memoriam along the roadway. Jordanian troops seized the historic Old City of Jerusalem, forcing the evacuation of the ancient Jewish quarter. The seige as such melted when Jewish workers cut a new road through the mountains, but Jerusalem remained bisected by a no-man's-land until 1967.

Arab armies came within ten miles of the Mediterranean, threatening to cut Israel's vulnerable middle. Outlying Jewish settlements were cut off and crushed. Egyptian troops occupied southern Palestine, while Jordanian, Iraqi, Syrian, and Lebanese units gained control of the West Bank and parts of Galilee. Then miraculously the outnumbered and poorly armed Israelis stiffened the line and held.

The United Nations secured a four-week truce in June 1948. The distinguished Swedish diplomat Count Bernadotte, sent as UN truce mediator, sought to devise a plan that would turn the truce into a peace. He proposed a Palestinian union that would include Jordan in a federation of Jewish and Arab states. The plan was rejected by the Arabs, even though it made them more generous territorial concessions than the original partition plan. Israel had suffered too many broken promises after the Balfour Declaration, and rejected it as a downgrading of the original UN promise. The UN sought to extend the truce; Israel was willing. But Arab leaders thought they smelled victory and knew they would have nothing but strong language to fear from the UN as they executed their own solution to the Palestine problem.

The truce lapsed and fighting resumed. Arab confidence proved to be misplaced. The energetic Israelis had consolidated an effective government under Prime Minister David Ben Gurion, established a unified military command, and—most amazingly—created a quartermaster operation that could supply the hodgepodge of equipment they had scraped up hither, thither, and yon. By contrast, the Arab armies were supplied with standard British equipment.

Both sides circumvented the truce provision that no new military supplies should be introduced. Even so, neither side could boast the most modern implements or ample reserve stockpiles. The Israelis proved more resourceful technologically, keeping their castoff equipment in operating condition and developing the rudiments of a native armaments industry. Among the more interesting products was the Davidka (Little David) mortar used in the defense of Jerusalem, where one of these is preserved in Herut Square. Some military experts believe it was more effective in producing morale-building pyrotechnics for the defenders than for inflicting injury on the enemy.

The tide of war shifted markedly in Israel's favor. Lod (Lydda), with its strategic airport, and Ramla, both hard by Tel Aviv, fell to Israel. Israeli forces also gained ground in Galilee, including the town of Nazareth. But the Arab armies remained essentially intact on the field. The Syrians and Jordanians proved particularly formidable. The United Nations managed to proclaim a second truce, which held until autumn, despite periodic violations. Count Bernadotte produced a second settlement plan, which would have permitted Jordan to annex the Arab part of Palestine and which basically sought to buy peace at the expense of Israel through enlarging Arab territorial concessions. Enraged Israeli extremists, probably Sternists, assassinated Bernadotte. The Ben Gurion government offered a considerable reward ($20,000) but the culprits were never apprehended. America's Ralph Bunche, Bernadotte's deputy, assumed the arduous role of mediator.

The last Bernadotte plan attracted some favorable international attention, promoting the not unjustified suspicion in Israel that the governments of the world might just be willing to sell them short for the sake of a little quiet. More evidence pointing in this direction has accumulated since. Among the parties to the war, only Jordan, which had a great deal to gain, failed to rejected the Bernadotte proposal.

The second truce broke down in October. Israeli forces swept back into the Negev, promised to Israel under the UN partition but occupied by Egypt. "Operation Ten Plagues" was a resounding success. Some young Israeli officers begged permission to sweep north from the Negev to clear Arab forces from Jerusalem and the highlands all the way to Galilee, giving Israel a defensible frontier along the Jordan river. Ben Gurion's civilian government vetoed the idea, since the UN was bending efforts to achieve yet another cease-fire.

Cease-fire came in January 1949. Israel and Egypt signed an armistice in February. All the maneuvering and shooting were not over, though, until Jordan in April and Syria in July joined Israel in signing armistice documents. Iraq and Saudi Arabia did not sign formal agreements, but they had no common borders with Israel.

The United Nations provided the documentary basis for the

Dr. Ralph Bunche, UN Acting Mediator, reads the Egyptian-Israeli Armistice agreement at the Rhodes Conference, February 1949.

rebirth of Israel. But the state of Israel was truly the creation of the Israeli people themselves, born of their own blood and travail and supported only by private aid from abroad. Israel therefore properly regards the 1948 conflict as her own successful war of independence. The UN proved totally incapable of protecting the new nation at its inception and frequently appeared to lack the will to do so even if it knew a way. It is therefore not surprising that the people of Israel were not enamored of the prospect of having their postwar destiny dictated from abroad by those who at best had left her in the lurch with no more than verbal support, and at worst had contemplated her demise with equanimity.

Israel accepted the various UN truces and negotiated armistice agreements under UN auspices although at the conclusion of hostilities her small but doughty army was in a position to gain more favorable strategic positions. Israel would not retreat from the cease-fire lines. These became the de facto borders of the new country pending the freely negotiated peace that Israel hoped, and still hopes, to achieve. Within her de facto borders Israel controlled the territory allotted her by the UN partition. In addition she held the rest of Galilee, a corridor to West Jerusalem, a bit more of the coast, and a slightly larger part of the Negev. The independent Palestinian Arab state evaporated as Egypt annexed the Gaza Strip, and Jordan the West Bank territories and East Jerusalem (including the Old City). Jewish pilgrims were callously barred from the Wailing Wall and other places sacred to them. Thus perished the UN plan for a neutral zone and for a Palestinian Arab sovereignty.

Among the most tragic results of the war was the creation of a mass of Palestinian Arab refugees. Arab sources numbered them near a million, though it is difficult to see how there could be almost as many Arab refugees from Israel as the mandate recorded for the total Arab population of Palestine, unless the British were grossly inaccurate. After all, the Arab inhabitants of Jerusalem and the West Bank remained where they were, and some 200,000 Arabs continued to reside in Israel. Israel estimated the number of refugees at fewer than 600,000. Yet even the smaller figure is appalling, and the human problem would outweigh the statistics if there were only ten refugees, let alone thousands. The refugee problem is of such import that I shall discuss it in a separate chapter.

The outcome of the 1948 war differed somewhat from the expectations of some cynical observers. Many had guessed that Arab military action would render the whole partition question a dead letter and permit the UN to salvage its moral reputation by bailing out a tiny "Jewish Vatican" around Tel Aviv. Dictated by the fortunes of war, the de facto boundaries of Israel presented a strange configuration and a continual strategic headache for her defenders. Economically Israel had her head just out of the water. Militarily her position was precarious. Generally her holdings were scarred by war and the unofficial strife that went before it. But after nearly two thousand years and against the most formidable odds Israel was reborn. For her people that was enough.

4. Arab views of Israel

The events of the late 1940's brought to a climactic point the process by which Israel became a fact of life after nearly two thousand years as a memory and a hope. Unfortunately, many of Israel's neighbors were resolved that the fact should be short-lived. It is misleading to speak of *the* Arab view of Israel, since Arabs are as disposed to various opinions as other persons. However, it is possible to speak of an "official" Arab view, since there are forces at work that militate toward uniformity of the Arab mind on the question of Israel. Propaganda from the belligerent Arab states, the Arab guerrilla organizations, and various external patrons of the official line have been consistent, insistent, and strident. Many Arabs sincerely believe they have been terribly wronged. They and their external sympathizers tend to be emotional advocates rather than rational inquirers. The innocence of their client and the guilt of Israel are assumed *a priori,* and accordingly every piece of evidence is warped and preinterpreted. The result is a dreary and repetitive exercise in circular logic. At the same time, Israelis and their friends have been known to speak and to act in ways that wounded Arab pride, reinforcing the pervasive negativism.

Finally, it is physically dangerous to express views on Israel which differ from the official norm if one is an Arab in an Arab land, and possibly for anyone anywhere. King Abdullah of Jordan was assassinated by a Palestinian Arab because of his relatively open stance toward Israel. The Tunisian embassy in Cairo was burned by a mob without police interference after President Bourguiba uttered a few halting and preliminary words in the direction of peaceful settlement with Israel. In Prague, an official of an American-Jewish philanthropic organization was murdered, it is believed, by Arab agents. Arab students with the support of anti-Semitic radicals have disrupted occasions when Israeli diplomats were to speak in Germany. Senator Robert F. Kennedy was murdered by an Arab immigrant after he spoke favorably of Israel's desire to buy American jet aircraft.

An extreme form of the official Arab view holds that Israel simply does not exist. An American tourist was shocked when an Arab border policeman scissored Israel out of his *National Geographic* map of the Middle East. Maps published by the Jordan government label Israel "Hashemite Kingdom of Jordan: Occupied Territory" (this might give pause to advocates of an independent Palestinian Arab state).

But even in the bizarre world of Arab politics it has become increasingly difficult to overlook the reality of Israel, especially since 1967. Hence there is a less fantastic position that recognizes that Israel exists but must be eliminated. At one time this intention was embodied in the boast that the Jews would be driven into the sea and exterminated. Lately this boast is seldom heard. No doubt it has been acknowledged that this task would be formidable. Probably Arab propagandists also recognize that the threat of genocide hardly advances the Arab cause in the minds of moral men. Yet it is not clear that the muting of the threat of genocide represents the retraction of the intention. Western apologists for the Arab side have been inclined to say, "I don't believe they would do that anyhow." One remembers that the same was said of Germany in the 1930s. Quite aside from the fact that it is demeaning not to take people more or less at their word (and not a little of the patronizing colonialist mentality persists among many pro-Arab Westerners), prudence dictates that a threat be taken seriously in a belligerent situation, especially when it has been drummed home relentlessly, even in elementary school textbooks, as a desirable and virtuous action. The threat is even more menacing when the enemy has given no evidence that his capacity for vicious action stops at machine-gunning civilian airliners at neutral airports and dropping nerve gas on defenseless peasants.

But even if the official Arab view has abandoned the notion that it is desirable to exterminate the Israeli people, the destruction of the state of Israel is still advocated. The more recent pronouncements of the major Palestinian guerrilla organizations declare that after the "liberation," native-born Palestinian Jews would be permitted to live in the Arab state of Palestine. Where the others would go and how many native Jews would survive to enjoy the dubious benefits of minority status under a Moslem Arab government is not clear.

President Nasser of Egypt is properly regarded as one of the most authoritative Arab spokesmen. He is among the few Arab leaders who could be expected to return to power with a large popular majority in the unlikely event of a genuinely free election. President Nasser's statements about Israel reflect a calculated ambiguity. The cursory reader or listener gets the impression of flexibility. He seems to say that Egypt is ready to negotiate a fair settlement of all issues once Israel evacuates the Arab lands occupied in the 1967 war. Closer examination, however, reveals a harder line. Israeli withdrawal would only create the conditions for negotiation. Possibly full repatriation of all Arab refugees would be a further prerequisite to negotiation. And what would be negotiated? Israel's occupation of Arab territory, which includes all of Palestine, according to the official Arab line. It may be that

54. Arab views of Israel

Israel is being offered no more than the choice between destruction on the battlefield and destruction at the conference table. There has yet to be a clear statement from a high leader of a major Arab belligerent that there are credible political and diplomatic conditions under which Israel would be accorded the right to viable existence. My own conversations with adherents of the official Arab position, ranging from official figures to private persons, reveal differences only in the degree of violence to accompany Israel's demise. The more humane foresee that Israel will simply wither by attrition, like the medieval Crusader kingdom. More typical is the statement of a pro-Arab American professor: "If they [the Arabs] can't do it themselves, they'll get somebody else [Russia? China?] to kick them [the Israelis] out."

The notion that peace can come only at the price of the existence of a sovereign state is a political obscenity little heard since Rome plowed salt into the soil of Carthage. Even at the height of World War II, when American emotions were brought to fever pitch by the sneak attack on Pearl Harbor and the revelation of Axis war atrocities, the possibility of eradicating the German or the Japanese state never approached serious policy. Rather, the question was how these states should be brought back into the family of nations. On what ground do adherents of the official Arab view conclude that Israel deserves such a unique destiny?

First, it is held that Israel was created illegally. Yet it is difficult to discover a newly independent nation with a more impressive pedigree, written by a majority of the member states of the United Nations on the basis of title deeds extending into the depths of antiquity. The existence of a number of the emerging nations rests on nothing more than the fiat of a former colonial power conferring sovereignty on a group of carefully chosen successor leaders (or a group of self-ordained revolutionary chieftains) to rule a gerrymandered territory that sunders all traditional tribal claims on a land where a recognized state never existed before. Yet no one denies the legality of these states. Rather, the majority of mankind wishes them Godspeed.

Second, it is argued that Israel's historic claim to the land is flimsy. Much scorn is heaped on Israel's appeal to biblical evidence. Some pro-Arab Protestant clergymen have gone so far as to assert that Israel's claims rest on nothing more than insubstantial legends from the tenth century B.C. How they square this assertion with the fact that they have affirmed before God and man, "I believe the Scriptures of the Old and New Testaments to be the word of God, the only normative rule of faith and practice" (or words to that effect), is not quite clear. In fact, Israel's historic land claims rest on a variety of evidence, of which the "promises to the fathers" are only a part. It would be useful to distinguish the historical claim from the religious one, though both are strong, simply to avoid confusion.

Historically, even those who dismiss the stories of Abraham and the other patriarchs in Genesis as legend would in honesty be obliged to confess that the legends (if such they be) witness to the historical fact of Israel's claim on Palestine. A jurist or a historian can ask no more, since God cannot be compelled to testify under oath and theologians sometimes disagree about His intentions. The Old Testament as a historical document, quite apart from its religious import, testifies to the Israelite claim to Palestine from the late second millennium B.C. (earlier, if Professor Albright's school is correct) to the late first millennium. The deuterocanonical books, the Pseudepigrapha, and the New Testament document the claim into the Christian era. Nonbiblical sources add further confirmation, and reveal, as noted in Chapter 2, that this claim was never renounced, but in fact has been treasured and reiterated across the centuries.

From the religious standpoint, Christian, Moslem, and Jewish traditions have always recognized Palestine to be the land of the Jews. American Christians, with their strong heritage of religious individualism and voluntarism, sometimes overlook the fact that Judaism involves not only a personal faith but also membership in a people and a devotional attachment to a holy land. The communal aspect of Judaism is becoming clearer to American Christians as they recover more of their own communal heritage ("the koinonea of the saints"). This has always been clear in the Middle East and other places where one's very personal identity is a function of his religious community. Christians who value pilgrimage and Moslems impressed by the sacred aura of Mecca should appreciate the religious force of holy land.

Arab propaganda, accommodating itself to Islam's tradition of qualified religious tolerance and the stigma of religious prejudice in advanced societies, has adopted the position that the Arabs are not opposed to Jews but rather that they are against Zionists. Professional anti-Semites have been quick to recognize the beauty of this distinction. They can adopt a cloak of respectability by opposing a political movement (Zionism) rather than a religion (Judaism). Meanwhile, they can conduct business as usual, since all practicing Jews are perforce Zionists, if only in an idealized and futuristic sense, and a majority of Jews are Zionists in the sense that they support the creation and success of the state of Israel and desire the right to visit the holy places of Palestine for themselves, for their co-religionists, and for those Christians and Moslems who also revere Palestinian sites. There is evidence that some Arab propagandists have not been above feeding the fires of plain, old-fashioned anti-Semitism. But the Jewish/Zionist distinction, however specious, seems the present official Arab view.

These considerations do not require that all Christians, Moslems, and Jews be uncritical advocates of Israel. However, they do point to historic recognition of the place that Israel occupies as a vital symbol in Jewish piety. It is as deserving of respect and consideration by non-Jews as are the symbols of Christianity, Islam, Hinduism, and other persuasions by persons outside those communities.

Third, it is argued that Israel represents an attempt to re-introduce Western imperialism into the Middle East. The fact that some Western states supported the creation of Israel and do business with Israel constitutes the only tenuous evidence for this charge. It is almost impossible to show that Israel serves any imperialist interest, but for one single atypical action: Israel did succumb to temptation and shared in the 1956 Suez conflict. She quickly recognized the error and has never repeated it. Israel has given no foreign power military

*Israeli school nurse treating Arab youngsters at Tirah,
an Israeli-Arab town.*

bases or military concessions on her soil (Russia enjoys such
privileges in Egypt and seems likely to gain them in other
Arab countries). Israel has joined no alliance or power bloc.
Oil is presumably among the prizes imperialists would seek
in the Middle East, and Israel's existence has made life more
difficult, if anything, for foreign oil companies and other business interests. Finally, Israel has resolutely pursued an independent foreign policy line and has been the client of no
one. She has steadfastly declined to be the uncritical apologist
of any alien interest, unlike those Arab spokesmen who
rushed to approve the rape of Czechoslovakia by their Russian
patron in 1968 on the ground that the Soviets were crushing
a "Zionist plot." Israel has been subjected to military threats

by Britain and Russia and economic reprisals bordering on outright theft by the de Gaulle regime in France. The United States—in some Arab propaganda the puppetmaster pulling Israel's strings—would be the first to testify that Israel does not accept dictation from abroad. Despite her weakness and vulnerability, Israel may be the most independent country in the world. (Since Americans ordinarily approve independence, hostile logic may find a way of construing this as proof that Israel is an American front.)

At times since the Zionist movement began, some Palestinian Jews have shown the bad judgment to engage in the sort of patronizing behavior toward Arabs that people in the emerging countries associate with the more benevolent side of European imperialism. Most often these "social worker" or Lady Bountiful gestures have been the products of ignorance, thoughtlessness, or misguided good intentions, but they have nevertheless produced understandable resentment among former colonials. Israel is not entirely bereft of ethnic prejudice, but what exists is minimal. Israelis in general are plagued by the fear that they might be prejudiced, concerned that Jews of European ancestry might be more privileged than Oriental Jews, and worried that they might not be treating their Arab and other minorities fairly.

Fourth, Arabs complain that they are being forced to wash Europe's dirty linen, that it was Europe's sorry record of anti-Semitism that forced the creation of Israel in the Arabs' back yard (or, as they would have it, their living room). This argument has some validity in that Israel's rebirth was accelerated by obscenities wrought against Jews in Europe. But it overlooks the persistent and ancient Jewish passion to return to the ancestral homeland. It is further weakened by the mass migration of Oriental Jews to Israel from Moslem Arab lands. The few Jews who remain in Iraq and Egypt would doubtless come to Israel, too, if they could get out.

Fifth, Israel is said to be a foreign European intrusion into Middle Eastern cultural life. It is difficult to see what this means. A majority of Israel's population consists of the Sabras (native-born) and Oriental Jews. The language of Israel is no European tongue but Hebrew, a cognate of Arabic within the

Semitic language group. Israel has gone to great lengths to accommodate her European immigrants to their Oriental surroundings. Israel's technology is, to be sure, Western, like all modern technology, although the Israelis have given it some interesting native twists. At the same time, the Arab states are rushing to acquire such technology themselves. Finally, the Israeli passion for clean water, streets and houses, green fields, forested hills, and free democratic institutions seems to express something universally human, not a European idiosyncrasy.

Sixth, Israel is said to rest on conquest and hence is illegal. That this was not Israel's origin has been shown. But even if the contention were granted, it is hard to see how it would bear on Israel's right to exist. For example, one might inquire into the origin of the Arab claim on Palestine. It is a curious historical logic that decries the most recent conquest as a metaphysical pestilence while regarding some previous conquest as an expression of the moral order of the universe. If the Arabs acted on the basis of their own logic, they would go back to the desert and give Egypt back to the Copts, Syria to the Arameans, Lebanon to the Phoenicians, Iraq to the Akkadians, and Palestine to—the Jews (and any Canaanites and Philistines that could be found).

A general application of the logic would, of course, produce chaos. Europe would have to gird for hundreds of millions of returnees from the Americas with the restoration of Indian suzerainty. But this would be only a temporary problem, since the Celtic survivors would doubtless send the Germanic interlopers back eastward. There would be a premium on proving direct Neanderthal ancestry. A cataclysmic collision of expellees east and west along the Urals or the Caspian would be a lively prospect. Such places as the Arabian desert, the central Asian steppes, and the Aegean region would become a trifle crowded, to say the least. Such considerations do not render conquest morally desirable, but they do call attention to certain historical realities that are often overlooked by superficial political moralizing.

Some would hold that the majority of Palestinian Arabs aren't Arabs anyhow, but Arabized descendants of the Aramean Christian and Jewish natives of the time of the Moslem conquest. This thesis introduces several interesting complications, including the question of whether those who renounce a tradition do not also renounce any inheritance it entails, and the question of whether the Palestinian situation is really an Arabic cause.

Seventh, there are Arabs who recognize the legitimacy of a Jewish home in Palestine but who would impeach Israel's existence on the ground that the greater part of the land within Israel's 1948 borders belonged to Arabs rather than Jews prior to partition. Advocates of the official Arab line have been quick to adopt this argument: The land of Israel must be stolen, ergo it must be returned. The argument tends to be used with purposive imprecision, confusing the land occupied by Israel in June 1967 with territory that was Israel's from the start. Israel has little claim on a great deal of the territory occupied in 1967. But the majority of Israelis don't want most of it, anyhow, and are looking for a graceful way to hand it back. The assertion that Israel has executed a theft can be considered meaningful only in relationship to the 1948 holdings until the Arab states themselves create conditions that would permit Israel to withdraw from the land occupied in the Six-Day War.

The truth of the case is that Israel has not appropriated title to lands and properties that belonged to Arabs in 1947–48. An agency of the Israeli government acts as custodian representing the owners of record in the case of holdings of Arabs who fled during the troubles of the 1940s. Income from the use of such property is held in trust, to devolve on the owners of record at the conclusion of peace. Arabs living in Israel continue to occupy, use, or dispose of their holdings as always, and some Arab villages, such as Abu Ghosh, are among the more prosperous communities in Israel or elsewhere in the region. Some Jewish and Arab property has been appropriated under law for public purposes or for security reasons, with compensation and, where appropriate, government-assisted relocation. Some Arab property in the 1967 occupation areas has been destroyed in Israeli counterinsurgency activities, an unpleasant but standard means of coping with underground

Members of the Israeli Knesset (Parliament) include both Arabs and Jews.

terror forces, to be found in the handbook of every army.

In sum, the theft hypothesis simply doesn't stand up. Some Palestinian Arabs have been separated from their property by the fortunes of war, a war they may not have desired, certainly a war Israel did not start. Israel nevertheless assures them restitution or just compensation when peace is concluded. In the event that Israel welshes on this assurance, it will be time enough to ask whether anything has been stolen. Meanwhile, Israel is obliged not only to keep an honest set of books but also to see that her stewardship of refugee property is beyond reproach. For example, the rents charged should reflect the going market and should be adequate to cover taxes, repairs, and maintenance while assuring a reasonable return to the owners.

Eighth, Israel has been branded a greedy aggressor state, thereby forfeiting its right to exist. No doubt the world would be more peaceful if aggression disappeared. However, the definition of aggression, as well as the identification of aggressors, is a curious business, apparently very much a matter of perspective. The record is plain that the Israelis did not start the 1947–48 war, though they were bidding fair to end it when the UN achieved a truce. In a very real sense all the subsequent fighting has been an extension of that confrontation, as indeed the Arab states themselves often argue. But if the engagements of 1956 and 1967 are isolated from the continual state of belligerence since 1947–48, it must be acknowledged that Israel did initiate offensive action, in the technical sense, on these two occasions. However, there were ample immediate provocations in both instances, as we shall see in Chapter 5.

Israel's plea of the right of self-defense is surely at least as strong as the Arab accusation of aggression. Arab legend says that Israel is greedily obsessed with the notion of conquering an empire "from the Euphrates to the Nile." The Davidic empire extended from the Euphrates to the Wadi el Arish (the Euphrates, rather than the Nile, being the biblical "river of Egypt"). But most Israeli leaders know the Bible well enough to be aware that the Davidic empire was overblown, unstable, and ephemeral, and do not even aspire to a complete restoration of the more compact traditional Israelite kingdom. In truth, Israel lacks the manpower and resources to occupy an empire such as David's, and both the Israelis and the Arabs know it. In the unlikely circumstance that all the Jews in the world moved to Israel, the Jewish state would still be underpopulated for such a task, would not really need any more land, and would still be only half as populous as Egypt.

Arab apologists retort in rhetorical tones: "Then why hasn't Israel withdrawn from the territory occupied in 1967?" The answer to that is obvious, and it isn't the one Arab propaganda wants. The Arab states won't let Israel withdraw. Israel did retreat from the territories occupied in 1956, accepting the assurances of the UN and of several member states. She discovered over the decade that followed that her unilateral act of renunciation had not mollified her antagonists one iota, that her security was not one whit improved, and that the assurances she had received were of highly dubious value when crisis loomed again in the spring of 1967. Now, for the first time, Israel has viable strategic frontiers. She proclaims her willingness to relinquish this favorable strategic position in return for a genuine negotiated peace. Of course, there are supercharged hawks in Israel, as in every country, but they are a minority and their minuscule cadre would shrink to even smaller size if the Arab side generated less tension. If the leaders of the Arab states really believed their own propaganda, they would long since have challenged Israel to meet them at the conference table, where her alleged imperialist intentions could be clearly exposed to international condemnation. That they have not done so is the most obvious refutation of the aggressor charge.

Of course, not all Arabs hold what has been described as the official view. Some think even less kindly of Israel. Quite a few others hold more accommodating views. Amir Feisal, son and deputy of Hussein, Sharif of Mecca, the leading Arab figure in the struggle against the World War I Axis, endorsed basic Zionist goals at the time of the Paris peace conference. In more recent years President Bourguiba of Tunisia and other Arab leaders have suggested accommodation with Israel despite the risk of saying so publicly. Arab and pro-Arab scholars outside the immediate region have advanced settlement proposals of fairness and moderation, even if sometimes couched among slurs on Israel's history and character. Private persons in and out of various Arab areas accept Israel's right to exist without turning quisling to legitimate Arab interests. The ordinary Arab is rather like ordinary men everywhere in that he may be fired to outrage by propaganda. Left to his own devices, he would prefer to live his life in peace with reasonable assurance of adequate opportunities and a secure future for his family. The ordinary Arab differs from many other ordinary men in his extraordinary sense of generosity, graciousness, and hospitality. The official Arab case against Israel leads the average Arab to behave out of character. If the aspiring statesmen of the Arab world could bring themselves to encourage the typical rather than the atypical aspects of Arab character, a long stride toward peace in the Middle East would already have been taken.

The official Arab case against Israel is not utterly without substance of a sort. But its telling points are scored on peripheral issues that do not bear upon the integrity, morality, or legality of the Israelite state. It becomes compelling only as an exercise in circular logic when its hypotheses are treated as axioms, thereby begging the question in the mad dash to a foregone conclusion (e.g.: Israel is an aggressor, thus an aggressive intent must be read into every Israeli action, therefore every Israeli action is proof that Israel is an aggressor).

Most educated persons about the world probably believe that a sovereign state, once recognized by the community of nations, has an inherent right to exist, and it is both wrong and dangerous to suggest otherwise. Certainly the notion that a sovereign state can be put on trial for its life opens a Pandora's box of disaster on the world as we know it. Given the shifting fortunes and frequent cynicism of international power politics, there is no way of knowing who might be next in the dock or on the scaffold, or on what pretext. (It's a fairly safe bet that some psychopathic cabal would be howling for American blood early in the game.) In the case of Israel, even if one grants the outrageous premise that a nation may be tried for its life, the evidence does not warrant an indictment, let alone a trial.

5. Israel on the anvil

Israel had every right to hope for respite in 1949. The struggle to realize the Jewish state had been uphill all the way. At the moment of apparent triumph, when the United Nations promised fulfillment of their dream, Palestinian Jews were forced to fight a war against serious odds, without tangible support from the UN or any of its members, in order to save that dream. Now, amidst the ruins of war, they faced the challenge of rebuilding a land devoid of extensive resources and scarred by the ravages of history. They confronted the task of assimilating the hundreds of thousands of remaining survivors of Hitler's terror, followed closely by over half a million immigrants and refugees from the Oriental Jewish communities in Arab lands, themselves as culturally deprived as their former Arab neighbors. Add to this the fact that

Israel's most vital institutions of medicine and learning (Hadassah Hospital and Medical School, the Hebrew University, and the National Library) were isolated and inoperable on Mount Scopus, an Israeli enclave surrounded by Jordanian territory.

Respite did not come. Israel's Arab neighbors were caught in a new round of the vicious reaction cycle. The existence of Israel was not accepted, despite the armistice agreements. The hostile phase expressed itself in border incidents and guerrilla activity. The guerrilla troops were commandos to the Arabs, terrorists to the Israelis. The more neutral term guerrillas is used here, although honesty compels the observation that the nature of guerrilla operations generally supports the Israeli terminology. Civilians and civilian installations were and still are the most frequent targets. The guerrillas, largely but not exclusively recruited from among Palestinian refugees, were equipped and supported without apology by the Arab governments. Jordan and Egypt were the principal patrons. The Gaza Strip was a particular objective, although guerrilla infiltrators crossed into Israel from all quarters. Israel held the host countries responsible, since sovereign states are supposedly accountable for whatever transpires within and across their borders, and the Arab states made no secret of their patronage.

When the UN proved unwilling or unable to do anything about guerrilla incursions, Israel exercised her right of self-defense in the form of reprisal actions against both guerrilla bases and military or constabulary posts of the host countries. The military theory of reprisal is generally misrepresented by journalists, who ordinarily interpret it as a form of juvenile revenge-taking. Since soldiers are also human, the process cannot be divorced from the desire to even scores, but mere revenge-taking is an irrational activity that often leads to disastrous consequences. Military reprisal is a rational attempt to exact a price from an enemy that is out of all proportion to the gains he may realize from a given action. The reprisal may seek to interdict the activity as well, but it is not the same as purely defensive activity (in which Israel has been forced to engage on a full-time basis). Defense alone has never been

Armistice lines and Israeli border from Spring 1949 to present

LEBANON
Tyre
Kissoue
SYRIA
Acre GALILEE
Safad
Sea of Galilee
Nazareth
Dara
Irbid
SAMARIA
Qal at el Mafraq
R. Jordan
Mediterranean Sea
Tel AVIV
Jaffa
Lydda
Amman
Jerusalem
Qal et ed Daba
Bethlehem
Dead Sea
Gaza
Hebron
Rafah
El Qatrana
ISRAEL
El Karak
El Auja
JORDAN
NEGEV
Quseima
El Ghanu
Qal at Aneiza
Petra
U. A. R.
(EGYPT)
Maan
El Kuntilla
Ras an Naqb
SINAI PENINSULA
Elath Aqaba
0 10 20 30 40 50
Miles

(Reproduced by permission of the *Institute for Strategic Studies*, London)

wholly effective against guerrilla tactics anywhere. Reprisal seeks to discourage what defense cannot prevent. It further ensures that a persistent enemy will continue to pay a high price for his hostile acts.

A curious attitude toward Israel began to develop in the UN even before the 1948 war ended, and manifested itself with regularity thereafter. The UN seemed unable to speak force-fully against Arab guerrilla activity, let alone act against it. But a loud chorus of condemnation arose whenever Israel resorted to force against her tormentors. To some extent, Israel's own forthrightness proved a handicap. Israel's re-prisals were conducted by uniformed members of the regular armed forces and the actions were acknowledged by govern-ment authority. Clandestine acts of sabotage and terrorism by disguised irregulars, coupled with official denials, could have spared Israel some of the criticism.

The composition of the UN itself was changing. The size of the Arab bloc grew as former colonial territories became autonomous. Other former colonial states sided against Israel for reasons best known to themselves, often in an obvious bid to curry Arab support for their own schemes. The Soviet Union concluded there was more to be gained from backing the Arab side; the bloc of Soviet puppet votes swung into the anti-Israel column. The Arab bloc had what amounted to a built-in plurality if not a majority against Israel on all ques-tions before the UN and enjoyed the backing of the Russian veto in the Security Council. This joint mechanism success-fully stifled any resolutions critical of the Arab side and at the same time facilitated actions against Israel.

This cast the United States into what press reports some-times describe as a pro-Israel position. Most often what the United States has actually done is to soften one-sided anti-Israel pronouncements to the point where the UN does not entirely destroy its own moral credibility. It is ordinarily con-sidered a victory for Israel when a UN resolution is only mildly critical.

These developments have given Israel an understandable sense of isolation and have produced the conviction that she

Children in many border settlements have lived in bunkers all their lives.

is condemned to work out her own salvation or die in the effort. Persons outside the area sometimes accuse Israel of being overly sensitive, impatient, trigger-happy. Such critics should try for a while being surrounded by active assassins bent on their demise year in and year out, with only the most tenuous and unreliable outside support.

Exchanges of gunfire between regular army units became a familiar feature of daily life along Israel's borders. These fire fights usually began with Syrian gunners on the Golan Heights or Jordanians farther south opening up on Israeli farms. Israelis were cultivating the land out into the no-man's-land between the armistice positions. Although they made good targets, shells were often directed at the more distant farm buildings. The resourceful Israelis armored their tractors, located nursery schools and medical facilities in reinforced bunkers, and carried on as near normally as possible.

Heightened bad feeling developed when Israeli patrol boats interfered with traditional Arab water and fishing rights on the Sea of Galilee. Both *kibbutznik* tractor drivers and junior military officers on the scene probably pressed Israel's rights under the armistice agreements further than the Foreign Office would have insisted they go. But given their threatened circumstances, anyone would have tried for the most generous margins he could get.

Arab governments insisted (and still insist) that the armistice agreements had not ended the state of war, a circumstance that was somehow supposed to justify all Arab measures against Israel but not Israeli countermeasures. There had been an Arab boycott of Palestinian Jewish commerce prior to the events of 1947–48, and this was extended during the armistice period. Arab states were not only prohibited from doing business with Israel, but were to do no business with foreign companies that had commerce with Israel. Some Western firms, forgetting their passion for free enterprise and free trade, knuckled under to the blackmail. Egypt exercised her sovereignty over the Suez Canal zone to bar Israel's ships from that supposedly international waterway and eventually extended the blockade to foreign flag ships carrying cargo to or from Israel. Finally, Egypt declared a blockade of the Straits of Tiran with the aim of closing the Gulf of Aqaba on the Red Sea of all shipping in and out of Elath, Israel's only sea outlet to the east.

Israel smarted for the better part of a decade after 1948 under United Nations indifference or unfriendliness in the face of the Arab denial of Jewish pilgrimage rights to the holy places of Jerusalem and Hebron, guerrilla raids and border incidents that were mounting in intensity, blockade and boycott, and the progressive buildup of Arab military power. (No secret was being made of the planned use of that power.) Israel was obliged to spend a disproportionate part of her limited resources on military hardware and to maintain her small armed forces in a constant state of readiness just to secure her borders and ensure survival. The reprisal policy was continued as the only counter to guerrilla activity short of full-scale war. Prime Minister Ben Gurion's cabinet had concluded that military action must be taken to break the Elath blockade, because failure to challenge it set a dangerous precedent. There was no disposition to rush the operation, however. Major General Dayan, Israel's chief of staff in 1956, is the authority for the view that a major explosion would not have come so soon or been so large were it not for the activities of outside powers. Prime Minister Ben Gurion did not believe in taking a lot of nonsense, but he and his colleagues were certainly not warmongers.

President Nasser of Egypt was disappointed in the summer of 1955 when the Western powers would not fill his entire shopping list for military hardware. (The Western powers were engaged in a conscious effort to prevent war by slowing the arms race in the area.) President Nasser turned eastward, where his wishes were quickly granted. Most of the hardware was nominally of Czech origin but the deal was clearly a Russian ploy. Egypt benefited from a long-term barter paymen scheme in cotton. The arms deal initiated a chain of events that culminated in the resumption of full-scale warfare a little over a year later. The United States was offended by Egypt's recourse to the Soviet bloc for arms, and Secretary of State Dulles unceremoniously withdrew American financial and technical support for President Nasser's most treasured domestic project, the Aswan High Dam.

The Suez Canal was owned by a Franco-British company, but it ran through Egyptian territory. President Nasser expropriated the canal, proposing to use its revenues to finance the dam. Meanwhile Russia rushed in eagerly to replace the canceled American technical aid for the dam. Some Western quarters continue to express amazement that Nasser acted as he did when the canal treaty was slated for re-negotiation within a decade. Such persons fail to recognize the psychology built up in former colonial areas by past indignities at Western hands or to recognize how deeply the fact and the manner of the American action wounded Egyptian feelings. Further, the dam project is the key to Egypt's future development.

A variety of proposals to protect "users' rights" were advanced. They would have restored de facto foreign control of the canal. All were rejected by Egypt as colonialist schemes. It was freely predicted in the West that the canal would collapse under Egyptian administration, but with the aid of neutral European technicians Egypt proved capable of operating the waterway at accustomed standards. France and England, realizing that they would not get the canal back by default, began planning to recover it by force.

London and Paris encouraged Israel to strike against the Tiran blockade and the guerrilla pressure on her southern flank. Israel had been unable to purchase modern weapons to offset the new Soviet-bloc equipment in Egyptian hands. Britain and France promised to supply the badly needed matériel. The European powers hoped to use hostilities between Israel and Egypt as the pretext for intervention to protect the vital Suez Canal from war damage by occupying the canal zone with their own troops. Israeli intentions were quite different from those of the European powers, and her planning was essentially independent. Her objectives could be accomplished apart from direct Franco-British intervention. Such intervention would simply make the achievement of her purposes less costly. Israel accepted the proffered alliance with France and Britain largely in the hope of having some real allies for a change.

Israel's own war aims were limited and respectable in terms of her situation vis-à-vis her tormentors. She sought to open the Straits of Tiran by occupying strategic Sharm el Sheikh, to occupy the Gaza Strip—a major hotbed of guerrilla activity— to occupy as much of the Sinai as possible (so, as General Dayan said, "if we have to withdraw, we'll have somewhere to withdraw from"), and to gain bargaining counters that might succeed in bringing Egypt to the conference table for a genuine peace settlement. (Israel believes Egypt is the key to a settlement with the Arab states because of her size and relative stability, and because of President Nasser's prestige.) Rather than the traditional "to destroy the enemy's forces," General Dayan's combat orders were "to confound the organization of the Egyptian forces and bring about their collapse."

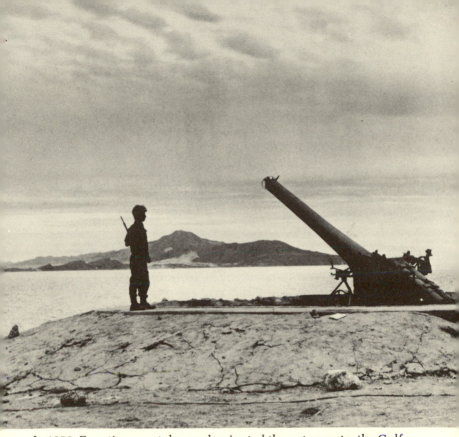

In 1956, Egyptian coastal guns dominated the entrance to the Gulf of Aqaba at Sharm el Sheikh. They were there again in 1967.

As he explained, "It is better that as little blood as possible should be shed." Even so, Israel's action was bound to be rendered controversial by the imperialists among her allies.

That things were not going to go so well as expected soon became clear to Israel's leaders. The eve of the Sinai War found Israel under threat of attack by her erstwhile British ally. Both Jordan and Iraq remained British clients at this point, although the United States was paying an increasing part of Britain's rent in Jordan. The British were intent on forestalling Egyptian influence in Jordan by introducing Iraqi troops into the country. Israel regarded the plan as a grave threat and suggested that her own security interest might oblige her to invade Jordan if the country were occupied by Iraq. Britain informed Israel that in that circumstance, British forces would defend Jordan. The issue became a dead letter when Jordanian parliamentary elections returned a pro-Egyptian majority before the troop moves could be made. Britain nevertheless continued to behave with suspicion toward Israel right through to the end. (British fighters prevented Israel's troops from moving to the immediate rescue of a downed British pilot. He had to wait for a British pickup.) France, however, developed genuinely friendly relations with Israel, which continued until the de Gaulle government launched a policy aimed at recovering French influence in her former Arab colonial sphere and the Israelis for their part demonstrated insufficient reverence for the grandeur of Le Grand Charles. At any rate, by the time hostilities were initiated, Israel was prepared for the contingency that she might be left to carry through to her own objectives without the promised Anglo-French intervention.

Full hostilities erupted on October 29, 1956. The Israeli part of the operation was executed with remarkable dash and efficiency. The performance of the Israeli army amazed foreign observers and even surprised the Israelis themselves. To be sure, there was the usual quota of blunders—the unit that jumped off too soon, the unit that got lost and missed its objective, the unit that took the wrong objective. Even so, delays in the Anglo-French intervention nearly produced a situation in which Israel had finished almost everything before her allies were off the blocks.

News of Israel's action produced consternation at the United Nations. Britain and France secured a recess of the Security Council, and before sessions resumed they were openly involved in the war. Britain and France issued an ultimatum demanding that Israeli and Egyptian forces withdraw from the canal area to permit a protective Anglo-French occupation. The demand was backed by the threat of force. The UN General Assembly (where France and Britain could not use their Security Council veto) came into emergency session. The Eisenhower administration indulged in a moralistic rage at having been duped by its NATO allies, France and Britain, and vied with Russia in arguing Egypt's case. At least the United States administration kept within the limits of ac-

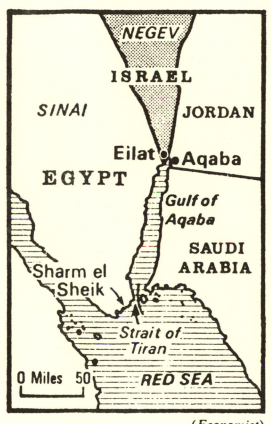

(*Economist*)

cepted diplomatic language. Soviet notes to France and Britain were openly threatening. The note to Israel was insulting as well.

Public opinion in England was anything but unanimous in support of the Suez campaign. Member states of the Commonwealth expressed profound displeasure. A combination of American pressure, Russian missile rattling, Commonwealth opposition, and negative British public opinion proved too much for the Franco-British alliance. They caved in and pulled out, leaving Israel alone. Interestingly, Israel had responded favorably to the UN request for a cease-fire before France and Britain decided to quit. Paris and London put great pressure on Israel to withdraw her acceptance, with the result that Israel consequently was exposed to the embarrassment of being the last to accept the cease-fire.

Israel stood her ground—alone, as usual—and refused to withdraw from Sinai until her oft-violated security was guaranteed in that quarter. Part of the guarantee took the form of the peacekeeping United Nations Emergency Force (UNEF, which will be heard of again). Neutral UNEF troups took up the policing of the border between Israel and Gaza-Sinai and occupied the former blockade point at Sharm el Sheikh. Another part was a promise to Israel to free navigation through the Straits of Tiran underwritten by maritime powers including the United States. (This too will be heard of again.)

Israel gained little from the Sinai campaign beyond an enhanced military reputation. It won her one ally, France, but the friendship of the French and Israeli people did not prevent the de Gaulle government from squelching the alliance (the less imperious Pompidou administration today shows signs of relenting). The presence of UNEF temporarily ensured navigation in and out of Elath and temporarily impeded guerrilla activity on Israel's southern flank (the guerrillas simply shifted more operations north to Jordan and Syria). Israel's most optimistic aim, to use her war gains to nudge Egypt to a peace conference, was utterly thwarted. The Arab belligerents again had their *deus ex machina* and Israel was condemned to another decade of what passes for peace in the Middle East. The neighboring Arab states continued to vow Israel's destruction and the Soviet Union continued to arm Syria and Egypt heavily, while the United States took over from Britain as Jordan's major arms supplier. The guerrilla war varied in intensity. Much more threatening to Israel's viability, the Arab states began developing plans to divert the waters of the Jordan River above Galilee, Israel's primary source of irrigation and drinking water. American-sponsored studies had recommended the fullest development of the water resources of the whole region for the mutual benefit of all its peoples. But the Arabs would have no part in a plan that allowed water to Israel.

Israel continued to struggle with the task of developing her lands, cities, and industries, and providing her people with a comfortable if not bountiful life. The burdens imposed by her voluntary task of absorbing approximately a million refugees from Europe and from the Arab lands and the involuntary necessity of maintaining strong defense forces weighed heavily on her energies and her economy. But for the private aid of persons around the world—not all of them Jewish but many of them American—her situation would have been even more desperate. Some of her Arab neighbors benefited from American and Russian technical, economic, and food aid as gifts or near-gifts. Israel by and large paid for what she received, did it herself, or did without. At the same time Israel dispatched her technicians and young people to the emerging Afro-Asian nations to help them master the skills essential to independent national welfare. The Israelis believe it is a moral obligation to help others as one is able, and that as people in the process of struggling to build and improve their own country, they might offer a special boost to those who travel the same road. After all, Israel herself is a newly independent state, emerging from colonialism and persecution.

Even pro-Arab writers admit that the UN and the great powers missed opportunities to move toward a resolution of the crisis during periods of relative tranquillity after 1956, when leaders on both sides might have made concessions without embarrassment. Apparently there isn't sufficient international interest in settling the crisis except when it heats up to the point of threatening world peace. Yet under those conditions, concessions by either side are all but impossible.

It is almost axiomatic that a crisis that is not intentionally cooled down will heat up again of its own accord. During the spring of 1967, Syria (which had acquired a government bent on outdoing the rest of the Arab world in its hostility toward Israel) informed Egypt that she was threatened with invasion from Israel. Indeed, Syria alleged that Israeli troops were massed on her border. Egypt was probably conditioned to Syrian excitability, but Russia (for reasons best known to herself) was moved to tell Egypt that her own intelligence service confirmed the Syrian report. Although UN representatives and foreign journalists and diplomats were unable to locate the supposed Israeli formations, the rumor had its desired effect.

President Nasser seems to have experienced great anguish over the fact that no other Arab state came seriously to Egypt's aid in the 1956 war. Egypt would never be so laggard under his leadership. Egypt officially requested the withdrawal of UNEF from frontier positions in Gaza and Sinai on May 18, 1967. Secretary General Thant obliged with unbecoming haste. Egypt, as a sovereign state, had every right to ask her international guests to leave. UNEF was located on Egyptian territory, since Israel had not begged anybody to rake out her chestnuts. That the guests were well advised to scamper before their usefulness as a damper on the rapidly heating situation could be tested is another question. Some sources not unfriendly to the Arab side have speculated that President Nasser did not really want all of UNEF to leave, or to do so with such rapidity.

The performance of the UN and particularly of its ranking official became a monument to weakness and ineptitude. President Nasser moved Egyptian forces into the frontier positions vacated by UNEF. Israel found that the UN buffer was an ephemeral thing indeed. She soon learned that the great power guarantees of her navigation rights were also of little tangible or immediate value. Egypt announced the reinstitution of the Tiran blockade on May 23. All the guarantors agreed the blockade was hardly sporting, but none seemed in a hurry to do anything about it.

Meanwhile, Arab propaganda boomed that the moment of Israel's extermination was at hand. The threat of genocide had not yet been muted. The Ministry of Religious Affairs in Cairo ordered Moslem leaders to preach *jihad,* ordinarily translated as "holy war," against Israel. Arab apologists are much upset to see *jihad* thus translated. They insist the Moslem doctrine of *jihad* simply refers to devoted, resolute, and selfless struggle. In the context of the Arab-Israeli conflict, the distinction seems curiously academic.

Both Israel and the Arab states mobilized military reserves, Israel experiencing what may have been the only 110 percent reserve mobilization in the history of warfare. Moved by deep patriotism and concern at the plight of their country, many overage ex-reservists reported to their old outfits when mobilization was announced. Algeria dispatched troops toward the east to aid the Arab side. Western nations were threatened with the loss of oil supplies and the loss of Western oil properties if they aided Israel.

The government of Israel, under Prime Minister Levi Eshkol, returned the national hero and architect of the Sinai victory, General Moshe Dayan, to the Defense Ministry in a move recalling Churchill's return to the British Admiralty at the outbreak of World War II. A man of independent political views, Dayan had parted ways with the ruling Labor party and had returned to farming. His appointment gratified those who looked on him as Israel's first soldier. It also signaled that Israel's ranks were closed and she was not going to tolerate mistreatment.

Defense Minister Dayan told a press conference that Israel welcomed all the diplomatic help she could get to achieve a solution short of war, but in the event of war Israel wanted no foreign soldiers to die in her defense. She would fight her own fight, if there had to be one. Israel was again deluged with admonitions to be patient from persons in the safety of the UN Building and of Washington, London, Moscow, and Paris —the standard prelude to criticism of Israel's actions in her own defense. The United Nations strove ineffectually to defuse the crisis, and Secretary General Thant embarked on a personal mission to the area. High figures in Israel's own government counseled restraint, hoping that American diplomatic explorations would point a way out short of war. On the Arab side, President Nasser told a trade-union federation meeting in Egypt that he felt confident of victory if war came, and if it came the objective would be to destroy Israel.

More than a fortnight of frenzied diplomatic activity elapsed after the Egyptian request to withdraw UNEF and the reinstitution of the Tiran blockade. Nothing was changed but the Arab military position, which was improved. War came in the morning hours of June 5, 1967. Israel claims she fired the second shot. Subsequent to the war, Israel produced documents in Arabic described as captured combat orders of the Egyptian air force and the armies of Jordan and Syria, which set forth offensive actions against Israel. One of the Arab batteries that regularly shelled Israel may have fired the first shot of the war. Egyptian forces were moving up on Israel's borders, whether or not they crossed them. The noose was tightening, and delay by Israel in responding seemed more and more likely to prove fatal.

The Israeli air force struck at the military air power of Egypt, Jordan, and Syria in turn with surgical efficiency. Israel threw everything into the effort. Only one fighter-interceptor was left at home to defend all the air space of Israel. Stratagems foiled enemy radar, achieving total surprise. The competence of Israel's pilots was amazing. Witnesses report no hardware was wasted outside the target areas. Even Israel underestimated the success of the air strikes. Arab air power was out of the war on the first day.

Egypt and Jordan collaborated in a deliberate lie, accusing American and British planes of participating in the attack. Israeli intelligence released a recording that voice experts identified as a conversation between President Nasser and King Hussein. The intercepted exchange revealed Nasser asking Hussein to go along with an accusation that American aircraft were involved and the king suggesting that Britain be included. The malicious falsehood was repeated by Arab organs throughout the war, and has never been publicly and officially retracted. Instead, the accusation was the basis for an Egyptian break in diplomatic relations with the United

The map shows Israeli day-by-day advances during the war in the Middle East. (Reprinted, by permission, from the *Sunday Telegraph*)

States and Britain in which other Arab states followed, for violent anti-American and anti-British demonstrations, and for an Arab oil embargo against the West. (Egypt did urge an American petroleum consortium to continue oil explorations in Egypt despite the ban, and it was done.) The big lie provided a salve for Arab pride by avoiding the admission that tiny Israel had eliminated nearly all their sleek Russian and American warplanes at one whack. But not even the Soviet Union accepted this one. She was in a position to know the truth. Soviet naval units had been shadowing the U.S. Sixth Fleet and would have observed any operations from the American aircraft carriers.

The intrusion of Soviet naval power into the Mediterranean since the mid-1950s had rendered the Middle East more threatening than ever before as the touchhole for an international explosion. By 1967 the size of the Soviet presence and the depth of Soviet involvement (artillery fire control on the Syrian front was said to have been partly in the Russian language) was such that American action in behalf of Israel would have produced a dangerous confrontation. The Washington-Moscow hot line was first used at this time under emergency conditions to avoid a disastrous miscalculation. The Soviets were informed of what was afoot when American aircraft went to the aid of the spy ship *Liberty* when she came under attack from Israeli planes and torpedo boats. (Israel paid compensation for the attack. That an attacking Israeli PT boat stopped dead in the water to offer aid when the *Liberty*'s flag was recognized supports Israel's contention that the attack was due to mistaken identity. American authorities have never given a satisfactory explanation of what an American ship, especially one of the *Liberty*'s type, was doing so deep in the war zone.)

The necessity for waging war on three fronts extended Israel's limited resources to the utmost. Freshly mustered reservists assigned to an undermanned line in the north were advised to expect no reinforcements no matter how badly they might be needed, because there weren't any. The primary effort was exerted in Sinai against the more numerous Egyptians with their menacing mountains of modern Russian matériel (including infra-red-equipped night tanks). Israel slashed along the three major overland axes toward the Suez Canal. Sharm el Sheikh was taken by a combined paratroop-amphibious operation that reestablished free navigation through the Straits of Tiran. Some reports estimated that more armor was engaged in the Sinai battle than in the great World War II battle of El Alamein. Israel's aerial superiority played a major part in her victory, Israeli aircraft exacting a heavy toll of tanks and trucks exposed on the sere Sinai landscape. Egyptian resistance was spirited, but the mobile Israeli columns overwhelmed the defenders of the Gaza Strip and threatened to flank and trap all Egyptian forces in Sinai.

Within four days Israel's army was in effective control of the entire peninsula and poised at the edge of the Suez Canal. Egyptian organization broke down in the field. Israel had more prisoners than she knew what to do with, but strenuous efforts were required to round up stragglers before lack of water and the Sinai sun exacted a greater toll than combat. Israel's treatment of prisoners was humane. The wounded got prompt medical attention, and many Egyptians were simply escorted to the canal and encouraged to escape home. Most of the demeaning remarks about the Arabs and their skill at arms have been made on television. The Jews of Israel know, from centuries of bitter experience, that when killing is done, it is human beings who die, whether they are soldiers or civilians.

The immediate nature of Egyptian intentions in Sinai during June 1967 may never be revealed. Expert war correspondents who viewed Egyptian positions immediately after the war found a curious mixture of offensive and defensive preparations. Some installations were pronounced textbook examples of Russian military architecture, not ideally suited to Mediterranean conditions. It is possible that historic Russian military experience strongly influenced the counsel Soviet advisers gave their Egyptian clients. The evidence suggests that Egypt might have planned to goad Israel into an attack, impale her on the Russian-style fortifications,

Israeli paratroopers at the Western Wall, June 1967.

and bleed her white in the vastness of Sinai. But the sands of Sinai were not the snows of Russia which trapped Swedish, French, and German armies.

Israel secretly communicated a promise of immunity to Jordan if she stayed out of the fighting. The Jordanian response was to open artillery fire on West Jerusalem and take the offensive. United Nations headquarters in the no-man's-land between East and West Jerusalem was among the first

Arabs from East and West Jerusalem meet after twenty years' separation. In the background is the Mosque of Omar.

objectives taken. Israeli troops soon liberated the UN and placed communications facilities at its disposal—generous behavior toward an agency that Israel had reason to regard as less than a friend.

In her planning, Israel accorded second priority to the Jordan front. Troops were shifted there from the Sinai front as rapidly as developments permitted, but the limited forces already on the line did not wait for help. The paratroops, some of Israel's best soldiers, stormed the Old City of Jerusalem with small arms and without air or artillery support, in hopes of sparing damage to the sacred monuments of three faiths. Israel paid a high price in blood for that restraint. Even so, the Old City was won. Jews had been banned from its holy places during twenty years of Arab rule. Not since 135 A.D. had its shrines been under Jewish sovereignty. A delirium of joy gripped not only pietists but also veteran soldiers (whose religious practice had been minimal) as they came before the Wailing Wall, Judaism's holiest shrine—all that remained of the last Jewish temple. Meanwhile, Israeli troops overcame the Jordanian defense, and the West Bank of the Jordan was under Israeli control before the last shot had been fired in Sinai. By June 8, cease-fire was in effect on both fronts.

Syria had claimed great military success on the northern front, although foreign correspondents could unearth tangible evidence only of heavy artillery exchanges. Swift success farther south permitted Israel to reinforce that sector. Defying all odds, the Israelis charged the Golan Heights in one of the most difficult and costly operations of the war. Officer losses were especially heavy, since in Israel's army leaders are expected to lead, and they do. For the first time since Israel regained her independence, the residents of the farms under the shadow of the Syrian cliffs could live free from the threat of sudden gunfire. The Israeli army was well along the road to Damascus when a UN cease-fire was proclaimed on June 9, to become effective the next day.

President Nasser suddenly offered his resignation in Egypt, renewing in the process the lie that Israel had been helped by Anglo-American forces. A massive outpouring of public emotion led him to retract the resignation, and some skeptics suggested he planned it so all along. The tragedy is that President Nasser's great personal popularity and obvious talents have so often been squandered on negative projects.

The United Nations exercised itself from the start to achieve a cease-fire in the war. A similar expenditure of energy months earlier might have averted the war entirely. Israel was subjected throughout the proceedings to the vituperation and calumny of the Arab bloc, the Soviet satellite bloc, and the Soviet Union itself, and to the evident unfriendliness of the secretary general. Foreign Minister Abba Eban, who had ably defended Israel in the face of massed Russo-Arab slander, finally made the definitive presentation of Israel's case before the General Assembly on June 19, 1967. Mr. Eban's rational, carefully documented address contrasted markedly with the abuse from the other side. Yet it is doubtful that his eloquence moved those whose minds had already been closed by dogma, censorship, and propaganda.

Israel took the measure of her sworn enemies in just six days. She had occupied enemy territory larger than the area contained within her own prewar boundaries. Then she stopped in response to UN appeals, though her army might have pressed on to Cairo, Amman, and Damascus. Similar restraint was evident when the early aerial victories opened enemy air space to unhindered intrusion. The normal theory of modern war would have dictated systematic bombing of strategic military targets in the major cities, if not of the populace. Lacking heavy bombers of the sort Russia had supplied to Egypt, the Israeli air force would have required more sorties than an air force so equipped, but it could have done the job. Instead she freely eschewed the opportunity to achieve a large reduction in the total number of her enemies. Such inviting targets as the Aswan Dam were completely spared. Jordan was offered immunity, and Lebanon, which settled for tough talk, was spared entirely.

Those parts of the world having access to reasonably free news reports were aware that Israel was genuinely menaced and faced possible extinction in June 1967. In some quarters there has been a tendency to have second thoughts in the aftermath of Israel's swift victory. Popular affection for Israel has always been stronger than official sympathy, extending even into nations with anti-Israeli regimes. Had popular will rather than diplomatic expediency and labyrinthine bureaucratic reasoning been followed in the major nations, the Middle East crisis would probably have been settled long ago. Some of the sympathy Israel enjoyed as an obvious underdog has, however, been undercut as she assumed the unlikely role of victor. It is worth remembering that the fact of victory did not turn David into a giant, nor did defeat reduce Goliath's impressive statistics. Both serious journalists and popular humorists have tended to demean Arab martial skills and to exaggerate Israel's military capabilities. Apologists for Arab extremism have been quick to jump on the bandwagon in the hope of gaining a propaganda advantage. The record must be kept straight. The truth remains that Israel is a small country of limited resources surrounded by an infinitely more populous enemy whose military desires are underwritten by Soviet generosity, by more modest Western arms aid, and by oil royalties paid to the economies of the West. Israel cannot afford a Pyrrhic victory, let alone a defeat. Her enemies have the proven capability to absorb the limited defeats Israel may inflict and go on with business more or less as usual.

The figure of 200,000 is often mentioned as the size of Israel's army. Even though this figure represents only about a third of the force that the United States put into the Viet Nam war, it should be noted that Israel's professional standing army numbers only 15,000 to 16,000, *less than the complement of one American infantry division*. The remainder of the 60,000 men ordinarily on active duty are reservists. The 200,000-man force (and part of the members of Israel's army are women assigned noncombat duties) represents full mobilization in a nation of only 2.6 million people. When 200,-000 troops are on active duty, Israel finds herself short of factory and field hands, taxi drivers, business and professional men, and university students. Conditions since 1967 have obliged Israel to keep about twice as many reservists on active duty as is usually the case, with all the hardships this entails.

By contrast, Egypt, with a population of about 26 million, numbers 180,000 men in her regular army and another 120,000 in her national guard. Jordan, almost as populous as Israel, has 50,000 men in her military. Iraq (population 8.26 million in 1965) keeps at least 80,000 men under arms, and Syria (population 4.5 million) over 52,000, including paramilitary police units. These numbers represent only the nearest and most hostile Arab states. Algeria, Libya, Saudi Arabia, Leba-

Russian-made missile captured in Sinai, June 1967.

non, Sudan, Yemen, and the Gulf sultanates have participated against Israel to one degree or another. Of course, some of Egypt's best troops were tied down by the now concluded Yemen civil war (sometimes known as "Nasser's Viet Nam") in 1967, but this was hardly Israel's fault. Arab apologists also like to point out that internal security requirements prevent the Arab states from putting as high a percentage of their troops on the line as Israel. This is an interesting commentary all by itself.

Israel has been obliged to purchase her own military equipment with a limited budget. There are consequently shortages and make-do adaptations, despite the considerable skill and technical ingenuity of native industry and army ordinance and quartermaster services. For example, a modified version of the American World War II Sherman tank remains a basic part of Israel's armored corps. The Sherman was one of the best tanks in the world in 1942. Again, though Israel's front-line air strength is made up of six squadrons of French Mirage and Mystère aircraft, and more recently two squadrons of American Skyhawk tactical support fighters (against Egypt's twelve squadrons of MIG jet fighters and five of Russian bomber types), she must jerry-rig guns and bomb racks on her slow and vulnerable trainer planes to muster adequate numbers of tactical aircraft in wartime. The heaviest losses in 1967 were among these improvised "war planes." The promised sale of two squadrons of American Phantom jets (replacing two squadrons of Mirages that President de Gaulle denied Israel without returning the payment) will hardly give Israel overwhelming air superiority.

The Arab states enjoy a much more favorable position regarding access to military hardware and economic considerations as well. Both the Soviet and Western coalitions have provided them with food, arms, and technical assistance, either as outright gifts or on barter deals and long-term credits. Major oil-producing Arab states have provided cash grants from their revenues to compensate Egypt for the loss of Suez Canal tolls and to support the war chests of the other belligerents. Arab matériel losses were being replaced by Russian air and sea lifts even before the smoke settled on Sinai. Fresh contingents of Eastern-bloc technicians were rushed in to instruct in the use of the new equipment (what else they may be teaching is a cause of concern to anticommunists around the world). A year after the debacle, Arab armed forces were better equipped than ever.

Israel hoped the swiftness of her victory and the magnitude of her conquests would bring the Arab states to a meaningful peace conference at long last. This might have happened if events had followed a normal course, but the machinery in the wings again created a friendly war god bearing Russian arms and Arab oil money. The belligerents had their *deus ex machina* to bail them out of the self-induced disaster and therefore remained confidently locked into their traditional response pattern of intransigence and hostility.

Pro-Arab publicists advanced the curious notion that the Arab states could not attend a peace conference as the vanquished, with Arab land occupied by Israel. One wonders how any war in history could have been ended if rules such as these were applied. Israel does not intend that anyone should come crawling to the conference table. She has given every evidence of generous intentions. Israel needs peace more than any other nation, and knows it will come at a price. It is not Israel but her enemies who refuse to accord the other side the status of an equal. The Arabs seem to feel, with some justification, that time and other powerful forces are on their side. Another confrontation between Israel and her neighbors ended in a diplomatic standoff with a tenuous cease-fire policed by United Nations observers.

Hopes that the tensions arising from the marathon crisis could be eased, and particularly that the Six-Day War could be liquidated, did not die. The autumn of 1967 saw a flurry of activity in the UN Security Council. Various resolutions were presented, and a British compromise document containing the salient points of earlier drafts was adopted on November 22. The November resolution provided for Israeli withdrawal from the land occupied in June, the termination of hostilities, the guarantee of the right of all states to exist independently within secure and recognized boundaries, the settlement of the refugee problem, the guarantee of free navigation on international waterways, and the dispatch of a United Nations special representative to the area to promote settlement.

Syria and the guerrilla organizations denounced the resolution, but it appeared that the other Arab belligerents and Israel would accept it. The Security Council adopted it by unanimous vote. Only its last provision has been executed to date, in the frustrating mission of Sweden's Ambassador Gunnar Jarring to establish accommodations between the two sides. That the resolution itself became a bone of contention underlines the depths of the impasse. The Arab states expound the theory that the resolution sets forth a series of staged steps, Israeli withdrawal being the first. Israel maintains that the resolution sets forth the proper conditions for a settlement that can be worked out in detail and implemented only by a peace conference. She implies that her diplomats keep a packed bag handy for instant departure to the conference site—this despite the fact that the Six-Day War left Israel in something approaching a viable strategic position for the first time in modern history. A Jordanian salient no longer extends across her middle to within fifteen miles of the Mediterranean. The guns of Golan no longer overshadow her settlements in Galilee. She has room for strategic dispersal of her aircraft. The Jordan River gives her a natural defense on the east. And, as one Israeli officer put it, whatever else one may say of the Suez Canal, it makes a fine antitank ditch. Yet Israel seems willing to barter away the greater part of this strategic wealth for a negotiated peace settlement.

Israel's desire for and insistence on a negotiated settlement sealed by a treaty or contractual agreement strikes as odd those who think peace is peace, however you get it. Israel believes, probably rightly, that a peace arranged or imposed by a third party or company of parties would not really be peace. The Arab states could always renounce such an arrangement on the grounds that it did not represent their interests and that it was forced upon them. They might be telling the truth on the second point if their Russian patron became sufficiently uneasy at the prospect of being led into an unwanted war by the next Middle Eastern explosion. A treaty freely negotiated with full Arab participation, however, would by contrast be the Arabs' own. It could be renounced only at the cost of admitting aggressive intent before the whole world. Further, in sitting at the peace table with Israel the Arab states would be recognizing Israel as an equal, a legitimate sovereign state. Israel treasures this minimal concession that she has never been formally accorded. Her adversaries seemingly remain loath to grant it.

The aftermath of the 1967 war has developed into a dreary replay of the two previous decades, with some of their more deplorable features enhanced. Beyond restoration of Jewish pilgrimage rights in Jerusalem and Hebron, about the only improvement over the pre-1967 situation, from Israel's viewpoint, is that most Israelis are now farther from Arab artillery. On the other side of the balance, Israel must govern and provide for the Arab inhabitants of occupied areas. The 1967 hostilities displaced additional Arab refugees, adding to a quota of suffering that gives Israel no delight. The Arab guerrilla movement has grown in strength and attained great prestige in hostile Arab circles. Guerrilla bases have been located alongside refugee camps, facilitating recruiting and propaganda activity and using the proximity of women and children as a shield against Israeli counterattack. The revitalized guerrilla movement has shown somewhat greater willingness to tangle with Israel's military than in times past. But its most notable exploits continue to be directed against un-defended civilian targets—a supermarket and an open-air market in Jerusalem, a bus depot in Tel Aviv, a student com-mons at the Hebrew University, a cinema in Jerusalem (where the bomb was a dud). Israelis have shown their solidarity and their contempt for terrorism by trooping en masse to the scene of the most recent incident. On occasion, Arab bombs have taken a heavier toll of Arab bystanders than of Jews.

All in all, efficient Israeli police work has kept guerrilla acts within Israel to a level Israelis believe they can endure for a long, long time. Arrests have been made in most of the major incidents. The occupied Arab areas have been amazing-ly quiet, owing both to Arab good sense and to efficient Israeli security. The uneasy peace has undoubtedly been mutually beneficial. Demonstrating schoolgirls have been the favorite cat's-paw of the Arab activists in the occupied areas. Border incidents mounted by guerrillas and regular Arab forces, often in conjunction, constitute a more serious problem. Israeli response to these actions has taken the form of routine de-fensive deployment and counterstrikes by aircraft. The Is-raelis have far from exhausted their options, which include large-scale combined operations to clean out particularly troublesome hotbeds.

A very menacing development of the post-1967 period has been a series of Arab guerrilla acts against civilian transport aircraft. Two El Al planes were attacked with bombs and gunfire on neutral airfields in Greece and Switzerland. An-other was hijacked. More recently, an Israel-bound American TWA plane was hijacked, with injuries to passengers and heavy damage to the aircraft by an explosion after landing. The International Federation of Airline Pilots Associations has been almost alone in taking a forthright stand against these outrages and the subsequent imprisonment of Israeli crewmen and passengers of hijacked aircraft. Of course, the neutral nations whose airports were violated were angry, but otherwise international reaction ranged from indifference to mild protest. The U.S. State Department managed what might be described as an apologetic rage when an American plane was victimized.

One Arab guerrilla group boasted of its depredations from headquarters in Beirut. Israel retaliated with a helicopter commando raid on Beirut's airport, which destroyed a number of Arab airliners on the ground. The Israeli commandos ran great risks to accomplish their mission without inflicting death or injury. A deafening cry of protest arose in the world press and in diplomatic circles. Israelis were frankly puzzled at the contrast. Apparently Arab hardware was treasured more than human life in international circles—especially when Western companies held stock in the Arab airlines. Arab terror bombs have also been directed against Israeli diplomatic and commercial establishments in Europe. Even in the United States, non-Israeli Jewish institutions have been advised to take security precautions against terror activities originating overseas.

Artillery exchanges have been particularly heavy across the Suez Canal, and Egypt seems to have written off oil refineries and other installations in reach of Israeli guns. Israel's finest warship, the destroyer *Elath,* was lost to Egyptian missile fire. Israel's helicopter commandos have executed raids deep inside Egypt, and Israeli jets have overflown Cairo, presumably more for the sake of warning than for any immediate result. Repeated shelling incidents and commando strikes on the northern Jordan front finally led to a destructive Israeli raid on the East Ghor irrigation canal. Israel agreed to a secret cease-fire arrangement to permit repairs when Jordan pleaded the sad case of farmers deprived of irrigation waters. As soon as the repairs were completed, Jordanian shelling and guerrilla raids were resumed as heavily as ever. And in a reminder that the Middle East crisis has more than local significance, intelligence sources report that Russian-made aircraft with Egyptian markings fly from Egyptian bases with Russian crews to carry out surveillance on the American Sixth Fleet in the Mediterranean, while Russian warships enjoy base rights in Egyptian ports.

Israel was reborn in a particularly uncomfortable position

95. Israel on the anvil

on the anvil of history. After more than twenty years Israel is still on the anvil. As the world enters the eighth decade of the twentieth century, her chances of escape seem remote even yet—unless one considers death a viable escape. Israel doesn't.

6. Refugees, Arab and otherwise

The Arab refugee problem predates Israel's 1948 war for independence. Palestinian Arabs had begun to leave their homes as a result of the unrest that preceded the end of the British mandate. These first expatriates tended to be relatively affluent persons who could afford to place themselves and their families out of harm's reach until the situation had calmed down. Friends of the Arab cause admit that their understandably cautious behavior deprived the Palestine Arabs of badly needed leadership. The actual outbreak of hostilities produced a much more serious situation. Before the war was over about half a million Arabs were refugees and their presence in the rear areas of the Arab armies hampered the armies' efficiency. (The "official" figure of one million presents some problems; see Chapter 3.)

97. Refugees, Arab and otherwise

According to Israeli informants, most of the refugees were created when Arab propaganda instructed Arabs to vacate Jewish areas in order to escape harm while the Arab armies exterminated the Jews, after which they could return to possess their own and the former Jewish property. Arab spokesmen insist the refugees were driven out with force by the wicked Zionists. Quite likely many simply fled the terrors and ravages of war, without encouragement from either side. Some probably considered flight preferable to Jewish rule, particularly in view of the horrifying terms in which Arab propaganda described the hated Jews. Some non-Israeli students of the affairs of the region suggest the hypothesis that large numbers of refugees were generated from communities that were centers of prewar terrorism. The statistics on refugee origins presently available to these scholars are inadequate to provide a definitive test of the hypothesis. But they regard as indicative the fact that the traditionally peaceful Arab villages produced few refugees and that most of these continue to flourish in Israel.

The fact remains that many hundreds of thousands were dislocated from their homes and property and exposed to resultant hardships and indignities. The lot of these refugees has not been a happy one. The great majority found their way into the Jordanian West Bank territories and the Gaza Strip, controlled by Egypt. There they became in effect the wards of the United Nations, specifically of the director of UN Relief for Palestine Refugees, who headed a hurriedly assembled polyglot operation, and the later UN Relief and Works Agency, set up to provide for them and, like most UN projects, largely funded by the United States.

The host countries have assumed part of the financial burden, although few refugee groups in history have received so much international relief. UNRWA reported the estimated value of host government aid in the form of services, land for camps, and security at $6.5 million in fiscal 1964 and an aggregate of $60 million from 1948 through 1964. Monetary contributions from Arab states totaled $12 million from mid-1950 through the end of 1964. These figures sound formidable, but UNRWA estimated its needs for 1968 at $47.5 million (contributions by UN members fell short of this figure). They should also be set beside the funds that the Arab oil states are contributing to the war coffers of Egypt and her allies. An Associated Press wire story dated August 18, 1969, estimated the war subsidy at $266 million a year—enough to underwrite UNRWA for five years, or to cover the $1 to $2 billion estimated ten-year cost of rehabilitating all Arab refugees in four to eight years, with cash to spare.

UNRWA and its predecessors established large, semipermanent camps to shelter the refugees in the areas where they had collected. The rows of monotonous barracks-like structures within fenced compounds are a depressing sight. They are hardly fit for human habitation, by Western standards. It is difficult to imagine that some of the residents of those dreary warrens were finding a better life there than they had known before, and certainly many weren't. However, for many others life there *was* better, at least in some respects. UN health and sanitation measures resulted in a higher rate of population growth than this same population had shown in the past, owing in large part to reductions in infant mortality.

In cooperation with other agencies, UNRWA sought to ameliorate the lot of the refugees through job training, work projects, and development projects. The host countries were never enthusiastic about the development projects, both because of their own limited resources and because of their view that the refugees were temporary guests. The refugees, in turn, were reluctant to put down roots because of hopes for restoration in Palestine. Not all the refugees, however, have chosen to rusticate in the camps. Many of the Palestinians, who were among the better educated and more sophisticated inhabitants of the Arab world, found employment in the host country or other Arab lands. Others emigrated to the United States and elsewhere. The presence of the refugees has changed the overall population of Jordan and at times menaced the stability of its royalist government. UNRWA has become—perhaps unwittingly—the servant of Arab propaganda against Israel. In order to ingratiate themselves with refugee leaders, UNRWA officials have permitted their pro-

Arab refugees in an UNRWA camp in Lebanon receiving supplementary food rations.

grams to become channels for the most violent anti-Israel indoctrination.

UN officials originally hoped for early repatriation of the refugees. Israel has always expressed a willingness to achieve a fair settlement for the refugees in the context of a peace agreement. As a gesture of good faith and through the good offices of the UN, Israel released some impounded refugee assets during the 1950s.

The refugee problem was exacerbated by the 1967 war. The majority of those in UN camps were located on the West Bank and the Gaza Strip, both occupied by Israel during the war. Many of those on the West Bank fled to Jordan; other West Bank residents joined their flight. Some Arab quarters accused Israel of chasing them out, a charge Israel denied. Given the anti-Israeli indoctrination they had received, the wonder is that all did not flee. Israel found herself the custodian of about half the original refugee group, according to UNRWA figures for 1967–68. The burden of providing for the refugees in occupied territory was increased when action by the Arab governments blocked the receipt of private aid from relatives working in oil areas who had formerly helped with their support. Facilities were quite lacking for those who fled into Jordan. Emergency housing was supplied in the form of nylon camp tents from the United States—remarkable contrivances, to be sure, but hardly suitable for long-term habitation, especially under winter conditions.

The refugee problem must be solved. This assertion is grounded on equally unassailable humanitarian and practical considerations. The sufferings of the refugees have been and continue to be both real and severe. The majority are innocent victims of historical forces beyond either their control or their comprehension. That some of their leaders have been in the forefront of the guerrilla movement, making settlement of their case more remote and difficult, should not be argued against the masses. On the practical side, no settlement of the overall Middle Eastern situation could be regarded as secure even if it were possible while such a large group remained unaffected. Meanwhile, the refugee situation remains a major source of discontent in a turbulent region.

It has seemed at times that the Arab governments don't want the refugee problem solved—that they prefer to keep the refugee sore open and virulent as an aggravation for future hostilities. One would hope that this impression is wrong, but only Arab government responses to future good-faith offers of settlement by Israel can determine whether or not the refugees are being treated as pawns by their own people.

In the past, Israel has repeatedly affirmed the position that she was ready to move toward a fair settlement with the refugees, but only as part of an overall peace agreement. It has been said that Israel should reexamine this position for more than one reason. First, the deprivations experienced by the majority of refugees are an offense to Israel's own high humanitarian principles. Second, the plight of the refugees constitutes a significant part of the Arab case against Israel (see Chapter 3). Third, a resolution of the refugee problem acceptable to the refugees themselves would eliminate a situation that is both a dangerous irritant and a serious barrier to peace. Finally, a generous good-faith offer on Israel's part would create a diplomatic moment of truth: the Arab leaders would be obliged to make either an appropriate response or a de facto confession that they were the dogs in the manger of peace. These have been the arguments, and clearly Israel herself has come to see their validity; for in his policy speech before the UN General Assembly on September 19, 1969, Israeli Foreign Minister Abba Eban recommended the convening of a conference aimed at settling the refugee problem without awaiting the negotiation of any other issue, "in view of the humanitarian urgencies."

The general outlines of a fair settlement are clear: compensation for those who lost homes or property, repatriation for those who wish to live as loyal and productive citizens of Israel, satisfactory settlement of impounded property accounts, and probably special payments to help provide a new start for those who wish to settle elsewhere. Funds might be required to help receiving nations absorb these new residents. The specific details of a plan and its application to individual cases will be more difficult. A balanced or impartial adjudication agency would probably have to be created to mediate between offers and claims within an agreed formula. A determination would have to be made to identify the genuine refugees (or their legal heirs), since UN officials believe that some are fraudulently listed on refugee rolls, while many legitimate refugees have never been recorded.

Precisely how many refugees should be repatriated is a difficult problem, because nobody even knows how many want repatriation. The official Arab position is that 100 per cent want it. Arabs have been offered a plan that would leave Israel's present territory vacant for resettlement. Israelis, optimistically perhaps, assume that only a small proportion —no more than a fifth—of the refugees would freely desire to take up residence in the Jewish state. They do suspect that the more hostile Arabs would try to pressure many more into seeking repatriation in the hope that they could be used to generate internal mischief. As a practical matter, no rational person could expect Israel to take in a large pre-fabricated fifth column. Belligerent extremists would have to be screened out. One Palestinian Arab immigrant scholar at a midwestern university (now an American citizen), who visited the refugee camps after the 1967 war, declared in a radio interview that the majority of refugees are not at all dogmatic about returning to their former places of residence. What they want is an equitable settlement. Here is another sensitive job that will require careful adjudication.

Some people have expressed doubt that Israel could afford an acceptable settlement. They are not referring simply to the security risks. The figure of $2 million over a decade has been mentioned, and this estimate might be on the conservative side. Prominent leaders of the American Jewish community have declared that American Jews alone would underwrite the financial costs of such a settlement, not merely as a form of aid to their co-religionists in Israel, but as a contribution to general human welfare and the cause of peace. The costs to Israel would be more than monetary. Repatriating significant numbers of refugees would expose workers and professional people to competition from the Arab returnees. Restoration of Arab property would displace Israelis from shops and homes they now occupy. Nevertheless, Israel professes that she is ready to make the necessary sacrifices. The only question is one of timing.

Many friends of Israel suggest that only half the refugee problem has been covered when the problem of the Arab refugees has been discussed. After all, Israel has absorbed over a million refugees herself. These Jewish refugees from Europe and then from the Arab countries came with no more than hand baggage, if that. Many were ill. Many had to be

Jewish refugees from Arab lands brought to Israel.

taught modern Hebrew. Those from the Oriental communities were generally in need of both basic education and job training. Israel welcomed all of them and provided for their needs. In the case of the Oriental refugees, no claims were leveled against the Arab governments for property left behind, nor was any other nation or international agency called upon to fill the gap. It has been proposed—though not officially by Israel—that the flight of Arab refugees from Israel should be considered an exchange of population similar to that which took place in the Indian-Pakistan partition and on other occasions in modern history. The proposal has sufficient merit to deserve consideration. However, Israel has sought no easy way out. She welcomed the Jewish refugees freely and without conditions. She declares her willingness to do her part in relieving the victims of the 1948 war, which she did not instigate. The good faith of this profession cannot be tested until Arab leadership shows a serious desire to achieve settlement.

7. Observations on Israel

One cannot be really aware of all that is at stake in the Middle East crisis without some knowledge of what Israel is like, for Israel herself is ultimately what is at stake. To put it another way, the land from Dan to Beersheba could sink into the sea and the mainstream of Arab cultural life would go on essentially unaffected (though one would expect many Arabs to mourn the casualties, even the Jewish casualties); yet the world in general and world Jewry in particular would be deprived of something unique and valuable, and the Israelis would have lost everything. One can get a fairly clear notion of what Israel is like from the uncensored media in the West if one does not stop at the stereotype of a picture-postcard land where suntanned *kibbutzniks* dance the *hora* with a shovel in one hand an a submachine gun in the other.

Israel *is* a picture-postcard land, but I must confess I've never seen a *kibbutznik* either dancing the *hora* or carrying a submachine gun. I did see an Arab Druze security guard carrying a submachine gun on a *kibbutz*—a precaution against guerrilla infiltrators. The Druzes, members of a heretical sect that split from Islam during the Middle Ages, have fought for Israel and have developed the job of security guard as a sort of tribal profession. They are very good at it. I know I wouldn't try to play any tricks on a Druze security guard with a submachine gun.

The visitor to Israel is impressed first with the people—their diversity, their individuality, their energy, their humor. An El Al clerk at Lod Airport jokes about the airliner recently hijacked to Algeria. The Arabs must move it eighteen inches a day to keep the tires from going flat. At that rate it will be home in sixteen years. Here is a country where people haven't forgotten how to walk—rapidly and purposively. It isn't advisable to get in the way of an urban Israeli who is headed somewhere on business. Or a *kibbutznik* volunteer pushing a wheelbarrow on an archaeological dig. In a very real sense, the Israelis are a frontier people, and this gives them a symbolic kinship with Americans, who are well aware of their own frontier heritage. The hills of Judah and Galilee are more sere and forbidding than the hills of Tennessee and Kentucky, and the Arab guerrillas are much better armed than any Indian Daniel Boone ever met, but the character traits of the settlers are very much the same: a passion for freedom and independence balanced by a spirit of unity and cooperation, a willingness to work, a remarkable energy, a contagious enthusiasm, a great capacity for friendliness and generosity. There are few other places where an American can be so tangibly aware he is in a foreign land and at the same time feel so much at home as in Israel.

Don't let the Israeli customs official stamp your passport if you expect to visit an Arab country with the same passport. An Israeli visa stamp bars you from most Arab lands. The civilized Israelis will give you a throwaway card with the Israeli visa stamp to carry in your passport. And they don't care what other visa stamps your passport bears. Prior to

1967, one could enter Israel from the Arab world via the Mandelbaum Gate, but traffic was one-way. Israel didn't make the rule.

Israel's detractors accuse her of militarism. In truth it is remarkable that a nation obliged to maintain such a high level of security can avoid the trappings of a military police state. A great hope of the Arab guerrilla movement was to break the Israelis' morale by forcing them into repressive police precautions. This hasn't happened, in part at least because Israel has one of the most unmilitary armies in the world. Where else would the officers give recruits an afternoon off from training to join them on a tour of an archaeological dig? The Israeli soldier again recalls the image of the American frontiersman. His professional officers may affect a guardsman mustache and a Sherlock Holmes pipe, remnants of British training in the Jewish Brigade. The ordinary soldier stands lean, hard, and tall, carrying his snub-nose Uzzi submachine gun unconcernedly, rather more interested in watching the girls than in killing people. They are good and they know it, but they aren't itching to prove it unless they are pushed.

Prime Minister Golda Meir has said she is glad Israel is a country that regards the loss of a single soldier as a military disaster. More surprisingly, Israel is a country that mourns the death of enemies, too. Israeli pilots speak in moving terms of their awareness that there were human beings in the machines they shot from the sky. Israeli soldiers confess a profound tension between the convictions they treasure concerning the sacredness of all human life and the necessity of killing to preserve not only their own lives but the life of their country. Neither their words nor their ambitions are bloodthirsty.

No country in the world offers a more vital example of freedom of expression, whether in the public media or in private speech. An opinion too outrageous for public print has yet to be found. Most of them sooner or later find their way into the "Letters" column of the English-language *Jerusalem Post*. Far-out views are received tolerantly. Most voices express their concerns in the mainstream of human attention.

During the summer of 1968, issues that exercised *Post* correspondents were the shortcomings of government services, low-quality standards in consumer products, the shortage of clean public restrooms, and concern over the abuse of Arab labor by Arab business in the Old City of Jerusalem (seven-day work week, child labor, etc.).

The craggy rock fortress of Masada has become a highly symbolic monument since its restoration by an archaeological team under Professor Yigael Yadin of the Hebrew University. There a handful of Jewish insurgents held out against Roman power for two years after the fall of Jerusalem in 70 A.D. When it became clear that the Romans would breach their fortifications, they took their own lives rather than be captured for slaves. Modern Israelis say, "Masada shall not fall again," and they mean it.

Masada stands in the bare, rocky wilderness of Judah above the Dead Sea. The official temperature is generally 110 degrees in the shade, but there isn't much shade on top of Masada. Professor Yohanan Aharoni, impressively competent archaeologist from Tel Aviv University, warns a group of American university students about the hazards of the climb by recounting the story of an Israeli student who tumbled off the Roman siege ramp and "broke both his legs and one of his arms. Fall off the top and we don't even come looking." One knows Aharoni would lead the rescue team if someone did fall. The usual course is to climb up the Roman siege ramp and after the tour climb down the precipitous "Snake Path." One day an Israeli entrepreneur is going to get rich with a helicopter shuttle for American tourists—"Tel Aviv Hilton to the top of Masada and return! Only 175 Israeli lira ($50 U.S.)." An American student who beat his friends to the bottom of the ramp runs from the lodge there with the news that Coca-Cola (new in Israel) is on sale and is ice-cold. For once many students pass up the excellent Israeli beer.

Prior to 1967, highway traffic between Tel Aviv and Jerusalem had to detour south to Beth Shemesh. Now the direct road past Latrun is open again. Israel is rebuilding the highway up through the mountains as a four-lane parkway. High explosives and heavy equipment rip through the rock in a manner worthy of a U.S. interstate project. But there are two places they do not molest: the memorial forest, where a tree was planted for each one of Hitler's six million Jewish victims, and the blasted and riddled hulks of the improvised armored supply trucks in which Israeli drivers tried to run the Arab blockade of West Jerusalem during the war for independence. They are national monuments, too, garlanded with flowers on the Israeli Memorial Day. If Jerusalem had not already been holy, the blood of these brave and selfless men would have sanctified it.

Jerusalem is the holiest city of Christianity and Judaism and the third holiest of Islam (after Mecca and Medina). Western Christians, especially Protestants, are apt to be disenchanted by the tassels and tinsel of Oriental piety. Petty squabbles between the denominations sharing the Church of the Holy Sepulcher have been no credit to the religion of *agape*. It took a papal pilgrimage to reach agreement on the repair of earthquake damage almost a half century old. Contemporary archaeology tends to support the traditions placing Calvary and the tomb here. One cannot be unmoved, yet one takes comfort from the angelic pronouncement, "He is not here. He has risen."

The area around the Wailing Wall has been cleared of slum structures and is being developed by the National Park Service. The stonemasons must adapt their techniques to work under the feet of tourists and pilgrims. Many come just to look. More come to pray. The fervor of the worshipers underscores the harshness of a policy that obliged Jews to regain their holiest place by force. The precincts of the Wall are officially a synagogue. In deference to Orthodox custom, the sexes are segregated into separate areas. An American Jewish lady must ask a Christian professor to remind her husband, lingering at his devotions in the men's area, that she is waiting. Those men who lack hats are provided with pasteboard prayer caps, but an old tennis hat bearing the marks of several seasons on the court and a summer of archaeology passes muster. Judaism is a religion of tolerance and assumes that the Holy One (blessed be He!) shares that virtue. A voluntary committee of pietists seeks to identify those who are Jews and to outfit them in proper prayer shawls and phylacteries, courtesy of the committee. An American Jew, obviously not Orthodox, requires considerable help to get properly vested.

The Wailing (or, more correctly, Western) Wall was built to support the enlarged courts of Herod's temple, the temple in which Jesus worshiped and taught. Solomon's temple and the second temple, built after the return from Babylon and liberated and purified by the Maccabees in the first Hanukkah, stood on the same height. The striking gold dome (a product of modern Italian craftsmanship) and blue tile (a tribute to ancient Arabic art) of the Dome of the Rock Mosque, standing over the rock outcropping that may have been under the sacrificial altar or the Holy of Holies of Solomon's temple, now cap the Temple Mount. Al Aksa Mosque, recently a bone of contention, stands to the south. The Dome of the Rock served also as a Crusader church—appropriately, since some of its materials were looted from ecclesiastical buildings. Orthodox Jewish pietists will not enter the Haram es Sharif compound, explaining that the former temple courts are too sacred to tread upon. Most likely that tradition rationalizes an accommodation to Roman or Christian or Moslem persecution in some distant past. The mosque compound remains under Moslem administration. Israel has assigned each shrine to the custody of the faith concerned and granted free access to the faithful.

Significant archaeological work, the first in the area since the British army engineers Warren and Wilson tunneled here over a century ago, proceeds along the lower west wall of the temple and to the south. Professor Benjamin Mazar, dean of Israeli archaeologists, directs the project. Some say international law is being violated, since excavations in occupied territory are prohibited. Jews cannot consider as "occupied territory" the city that David won, the city where Hezekiah ruled and Isaiah preached, the city to which Ezra and Nehemiah returned, the city that Judah the Maccabee liberated. Long-buried Herodian masonry like that of the Western Wall, a colonnade, has been uncovered. A glance upward reveals that Arab or Turkish masons incorporated Herodian column drums in the upper walls. Every Holy Land archaeologist dreams of digging in the compound at the top, but Moslem religious sensibilities have not adjusted to scientific archaeology and would be too deeply offended.

Everybody mixes in the Old City and everybody gets along. An interesting religio-economic synergism functions in Jerusalem. Arab shops close on Friday, Jewish shops on Saturday, and Christian shops on Sunday. Everybody gets a day off and practically nobody gains an economic advantage, though the Jewish shopkeeper can't profit from the droves of Israelis who pour in on their common day of rest. A Jewish pietist passes alone down the narrow streets (more like halls and stairways) on his way to pray at the Wall near midnight. He will complete the trip in safety. An American visitor compares notes with those of a pre-1967 visit. The streets seem cleaner and there are fewer police about. *Menoroth* are featured alongside *kaffiyeh* and crucifixes on King David Street. The bazaars require all the senses, including smell, to be fully appreciated. An Arab dealer in antiquities does not consider a transaction complete until the customer has been served tea or Turkish coffee. There are no more gracious people on earth than one finds in Arab and Jewish Jerusalem. One is convinced these people could live together in harmony if left to themselves.

The Arabs of the Old City are not enchanted by Israeli rule. Jordanian rule did not enchant them either. An Arab shopkeepers' strike is called to protest a near-riot following a terrorist incident (the Israeli police and army moved in to protect Arab Jerusalem). The strike is 60 to 75 percent effective at midmorning, 100 percent by noon. A committee has made the rounds. Israeli police take precautions but keep calm. Don't the officers on the corner know that fellow over there has an American-made .38 revolver in his pocket? Probably so, but they're here to prevent incidents, not create them. (One detects a rising sense of tension as one moves from Old Jerusalem to the new Arab East Jerusalem to the West Bank. Nablus is especially warm. News reports confirm intuition.)

You never can tell by looking at him whether the policeman in Jerusalem is a Jew or an Arab. The *Jerusalem Post* commented that the underworld was the first institution to "integrate" after the Six-Day War. The police had to be the second.

Sections of East Jerusalem are as modern, clean, and gracious as the best parts of West Jerusalem. Nobody begrudges this. Construction booms on both sides. Israel is preparing to reopen the humanitarian institutions on Mount Scopus. The old Hebrew University campus is needed to relieve crowding on the new campus, where construction can't keep up with the thirst for learning. The Mount Scopus Hadassah Hospital will probably benefit the Arabs of East Jerusalem more than anyone else. Israel has extended state-supported health services to all Jerusalem, but it's a long bus ride from the east to new Hadassah (built when the original was blockaded). New Hadassah is a modern, advanced institution, comparing favorably with American university hospitals. The American Jewish women who have supported it can be proud of their handiwork. The famous Chagall windows adorn the chapel at Hadassah. Panels damaged by a shell in 1967 are slated to be replaced.

Israel inherited some substantial but unimaginative public buildings from the mandate period. For over a decade after 1948, the influx of refugees forced a resort to hurried and economical construction, and it shows. Now the shortage is being reduced and Israel can try her hand at more leisurely and substantial projects. This shows, too, in imaginative new buildings adapted to their environment and in thoughtful new plans for functional towns on sites unoccupied since antiquity.

Archaeology is a national passion. Just say, "I was digging with So-and-so at Such-and-such," and all doors open. Everyone wants to know what you found, and will listen endlessly. But be careful of what you say—your listeners may have dug on the same site earlier in the season or last year. Israeli farmers take a vacation from cultivating in the hot Mediterranean sun by going on an archaeological expedition and digging in the sun. Even mad dogs and Englishmen know better than to try to keep up with them.

A bright lady army corporal expresses surprise that so many Americans, Jews and Christians, profess to be religious.

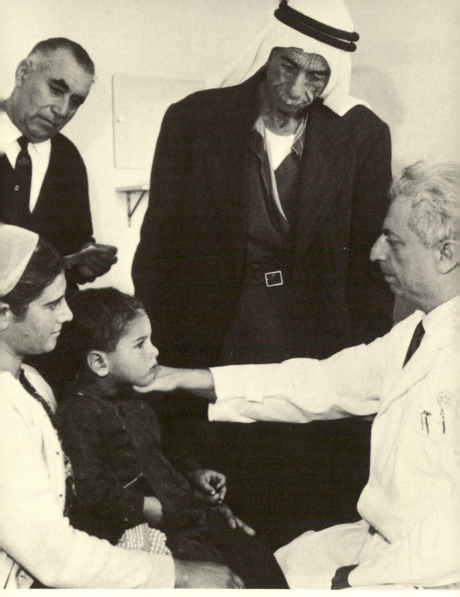

Arabs from West Bank receiving treatment at Hadassah Hospital in Jerusalem.

How can this be in the modern world? It develops that, for her, being religious means practicing an eighteenth-century Orthodoxy. Israel guarantees religious freedom to all persuasions, but Orthodoxy is the established church. Conservative, Reform, and Reconstructionist rabbis from America aren't acknowledged freely in Israel. Still, the United States' Hebrew Union College (Reform) maintains a handsome Biblical and Archaeological School on King David Street in Jerusalem. Many HUC graduates now spend a year living and studying in Israel. Those I have talked with found the experience vital and revelatory, both for their personal faith and for their ministry. One is obliged to feel that Israel's religious life would be more vital if Judaism's historic pluralism were given more encouragement. A historian is constrained to recall that in one of Judaism's most creative epochs the disciples of the Pharisaic rabbis Hillel and Shammai could agree to disagree among themselves and yet reach accord on straightening out the Sadducean high priesthood (while upholding their priestly legitimacy). Hillelite, Shammaite, and Sadduccee could share suspicion of the Zealots. At the same time, a young rabbi from Nazareth could preach a more tolerant understanding of the Heavenly Father's purposes than some would allow. And the men of Qumran could regard all the uplanders as apostates.

Part of the standard case for Israel is that it is more than the essential assured refuge. It is also the place where a full Jewish life can be lived, where being Jewish does not set one apart from the mainstream of society, where things Jewish can be taken for granted. An important part of the full Jewish life is freedom from the coercion that has dogged the community from the fall of the Second Commonwealth. Jewish tolerance and good sense have resisted ultra-Orthodox pressures to coerce Jewish conscience in Israel. The goal of permitting the full Jewish life in Israel would be even better served by the positive step of officially recognizing the inherent and rich variety of Judaism *de jure* as well as *de facto*. Israel already has variety. Judaism always had it. Why not admit it is authentically Jewish?

One ultra-Orthodox sect in Jerusalem does not recognize the state of Israel because it was not established by the Messiah. Scheduled buses don't run on the Sabbath, but chartered buses and taxis and private cars do. An Israeli Sabbath re-

Chemistry lab in a kibbutz high school.

minds one of an American Sunday, both a day of worship and a busy day at the beaches and parks. Some Orthodox object to the compromise. Ash trays in the King David dining room on the Sabbath became a *cause célèbre*.

There is enough that is 100 percent kosher in Israel to take care of all the Orthodoxy in the world. But overall, Israel is rather like the kosher food department in a midwestern supermarket: some kosher, some kosher style, and some spillover from nearby shelves. You can find pork, but it may be called "white steak." Most *kibbutzim* are notoriously easygoing about the kosher sanctions—although there are a number of Orthodox ones. It sometimes seems that just being a *kibbutznik* is a religion in itself. Not a new and different religion, but one of the flourishing varieties of Judaism.

The *kibbutz*, a voluntary, collective agricultural settlement in which all property is held in common, is perhaps Israel's most distinctive institution. No other people in the modern world have been able to make communal agriculture work so well. Maybe the other social experimenters emphasized doctrine too much and humanity too little. The utopian founders of the *kibbutz* movement didn't construct Everyman's Utopia, but they came closer than most. A *kibbutz* is really more than an institution. It's a great big family, a fact that some outsiders fail to grasp. The thing to remember when you're a guest of a *kibbutz* is that you're visiting in the household of a large, friendly, generous, helpful, hospitable family. But even if you're a relative, you're still a visitor and not a member of the household. Please remember that, as in any household, some of the members are going to be more and some less jealous of family secrets and private customs. Some *kibbutzim* have diversified their operations far beyond simple farming and most try to be as self-sufficient as feasible. In any case, all the wealth belongs to everybody. Another arrangement is the *moshav,* a cooperative of families maintaining their own households but sharing the costs and benefits of heavy equipment and mutual aid. In addition, of course, Israel has many private farms, operating as private farms do in the United States or anywhere else.

Some American reporters have suggested that Israelis are showing the strain of over two decades of tension, getting jumpy and hostile. I found the evidence for this tenuous. Israelis evince some of the typical Mediterranean excitability to which Americans and northern Europeans like to imagine they are immune. If there is a less hostile, less warlike people, I'd like to know them. The Israeli would rather go to the beach at Ashkelon than tread the fields of glory. Sometimes the beach at Ashkelon looks as if everybody in Israel gratified the preference at once. Most Israelis seem to regard fighting as distasteful. Being sensible people, when there has to be a fight they go at it with method and determination to get it over quickly and get back to the beach at Ashkelon.

There is surprisingly little bitterness toward Arabs even after the years of war and terrorism. Many Israelis have

Arab friends, not all of them Israeli Arabs. Some old friend-ships in Jerusalem survived to flower again when the twenty-year-old barbed wire came down in 1967. The Hebrew University has one of the finest departments of Arabic studies anywhere (specializing in literature and art, not social studies with application to military intelligence). President Nasser wouldn't win a popularity contest, though many comment favorably on his domestic programs to improve the lot of the Egyptian people. King Hussein is more apt to draw a shrug. "Which Hussein?" they want to know. "The pro-Western moderate of the American press or the gallant Arab warrior of his home-front propaganda?"

The ordinary Israeli, the worker, the *kibbutznik,* the bus or taxi driver, the lounger sipping the excellent local citrus soft drink in a refreshment parlor, is not dogmatic about negotiating positions. He and his wife would go along with any reasonable settlement that promised Israel a dividend of peace from her investment in blood and toil. The understandable hostility toward Germany has faded with time, leaving Israelis remarkably free of hatred. The Israelis' nerve and humor are holding up well. They can carry on for a long time just as they have been doing. They have lived so long with danger that the haunting presence doesn't disturb their normal pursuits. They may be in the situation of people who live near the streetcar line and learn to sleep through the racket. One day the trolleys are replaced by buses and the silence keeps them awake.

These remarkable folk deserve the chance to wake up one night in a world where it is safe to be an Israeli.

8. Prospects for the future

What does the future hold for the Middle East?

Only one fact is certain: Israel cannot end the crisis alone. She lacks the power and resources to destroy her antagonists even if she wanted to do so, which she does not. The basic Israeli attitude was summed up in the amnesty offered Jordan. It was confirmed by the lack of hostile action against Lebanon, which settled for verbal support of the Arab cause in 1967. (By contrast, subsequent Lebanese toleration of mass guerrilla operations has drawn recent Israeli response.)

There are two unhappy options facing Israel under the present dispensation. She can heed the Arab bloc and its vocal advocates within and without the UN, eschew her right of self-defense, and bare her breast (and back and sides) to the knives of her foes. Or she can continue her policy of limited self-defense, enduring the opposition in the UN and the nervous equivocations of her supposed friends. Since the first is unthinkable, the second becomes necessary.

How long can it go on? No one really knows. The power of the Arab states grows apace. Israel's economy has survived crushing burdens so far, but it could sag before the military balance shifts hopelessly against her. Independent Israel endured genuine economic hardships from a planned deflation designed to strengthen her economy in 1966, while urban areas of neighboring Jordan prospered with American aid. The most optimistic Israelis say they can hold the line forever, but a generation is a more common guess. A decade, barring some unpredictable development, does not represent preposterous pessimism. The Israelis will be holding the line against far superior power and population by guts and imagination. They must avoid expensive victories as carefully as defeats. They must keep up their guard against a surprise attack that could cancel all bets. Ten to forty years—maybe less than ten—remain for the world to resolve a situation that will otherwise burden whatever conscience it has left with the death of a nation and its people and a goodly number of its enemies, for Israel will not die easily.

There are two ways out of the impasse: international action, and a change of policy on the part of Arab leadership. International action is a fey hope. The United Nations was founded on the dream that it would be the impartial arbiter of tension and dispute. It can so function and has done so in those areas where powerful members or a large number of weaker ones had no strongly selfish interests to gratify. Where such interests are present, the UN reflects the cynicism of international power politics. The Middle East offers many temptations to these interests. Such a situation works against Israel, since she is only one—small, weak, poor—with only friendship and moral considerations to offer. The Arabs are numerous, control great resources of oil and govern the pipelines that carry it, own the Suez

Canal, possess a block of votes in the UN, and consequently can offer many tangible rewards.

One observes such situations as India, the world's leading political moralizer, applying rather different values in the Middle East than in Kashmir. India criticizes Israel and thus courts Arab support in her dispute with Moslem Pakistan. Russia abandons her brief sympathy for Israel and gratifies at one stroke her ancient passion to be a Mediterranean power, her historic anti-Semitism, and her strategic desire to undercut NATO's southern flank. The Soviet-bloc states have generally followed Russia's lead in their stance toward Israel. Notable exceptions were Czechoslovakia, which developed normal relations with Israel during her tragically short-lived liberal period, and courageous Romania, which withstood Russian pressure to break relations with Israel in 1967.

Israel confronts another international problem that has been clearly defined by Mrs. Meir. The Arab states have friends who are enemies of Israel. Israel has friends who also try to be friends of the Arab states. This is not surprising. The most powerful of Israel's friends are the great humanitarian democracies. Israel is tolerant and understanding of the desire of the United States and others to enjoy amicable relations with both sides in the crisis. Israel would like to make friends of the Arabs, too. Israel's own foreign policy has aimed at normal friendly diplomatic and commercial relations all over the world, not the creation of an Israeli bloc. Meanwhile, the Arab bloc has sought to forge a tightening ring of hostility around Israel. When Governor Scranton proposed that the United States pursue a more "even-handed" policy in the Middle East, Arab hopes for a strongly anti-Israel turn by the new Nixon administration were raised.

American policy has been pretty even-handed all along, even if at times more than a trifle inept. Even so, Arab mythology embodies the contradictory view that the United States is at one and the same time the imperialist puppet-master pulling Israel's strings and the dupe of a Zionist conspiracy. The first half of the fairy tale is contradicted by the independence of the policies of the United States and Israel, which sometimes are at loggerheads. The second half is equally a fabrication. The U.S. State Department has often been less than friendly toward Israel. Powerful oil interests have influenced U.S. policy in a pro-Arab direction. Anti-Semitic publicists and organizations with institutional vested interests in the region loose a regular drumfire of propaganda against Israel in the public press and their own publications. (Since the free public press in America has not lent its editorial pages to the official Arab propaganda line, Arab sympathizers cry that it is controlled by Zionists.) Back in the days of CIA subsidies, at least one pro-Arab foundation was underwritten by unsuspecting U.S. taxpayers. The United States had sold arms to Israel only in the role of supplier of last resort, and then only in types and quantities to permit a precarious balance with the Arab states. Meanwhile, U.S. taxpayers were financing arms shipments to Jordan.

The truth of the matter is that U.S. policy would be less even-handed and more pro-Israel if the nation's administrations executed the popular will. Americans admire Israel's courage, hard work, self-reliance, and love of freedom. Americans like Arabs, too, but they become antagonized by the petulance and the dog-in-the-manger attitude of too many Arab leaders, and they get tired of being called names and having American institutions made the targets of mob attack. The even-handed restraint of official policy would doubtless be the wiser and mutually more beneficial course if it could be made to work. Unfortunately, it seems that the United States could convince Arab officials of a desire to be their friends only by becoming extremely hostile to Israel.

What could outside powers do to deal with the crisis if they would?

They could intervene with force on one side or the other, a circumstance likely to trigger wider conflict. Such action would be desirable only in *extremis,* to prevent wanton slaughter of the type that has been threatened against, but never by, Israel. All parties and potential parties have a strong interest in avoiding a situation that would widen the conflict; hence the urgency of formulating other policies.

The concourse of powers could enforce a genuine arms blockade on the area and allow the situation to unwind of its own accord. This solution would incline the balance in Israel's favor for some years to come, since her technical expertise has made her modestly self-sufficient in all but the more sophisticated arms or those requiring a massive base of heavy industry. Israel would probably welcome an opportunity to scale down the counterproductive expenditures required to support a domestic arms industry as well as to correct the economic distortions occasioned by the necessity for overseas arms purchases and the maintenance of adequate security since 1948. The psychological impact of an effective embargo would overshadow the practical military effect. The Arab leaders might turn much more seriously to a quest for peaceful settlement if they were really convinced that they no longer had a *deus ex machina.*

There is an outside chance an embargo could trigger an all-out military assault by the Arab states aimed at winding up the situation before their last shipment of foreign weaponry lost its edge. There is a much greater chance the embargo wouldn't work anyhow. The lure of Arab oil money would certainly tempt the ingenuity of private arms dealers to circumvent the governmental restraints. The prospect that such an embargo might be instituted is in any case remote, now that the cold war has been injected into the region. The Western powers managed to keep the situation dampened up to 1956 by enforcing a relative arms balance. Russia's entry as an arms supplier in 1956 made it a new ball game. Now the fratricidal rivalry between Russia and China in the Communist camp renders it unlikely that Russia would provide an opening for Chinese influence by joining the West in an arms embargo. The main-line Arab leaders have avoided biting the Soviet hand that has fed them so generously, but they might join the more radical Arab leaders in an appeal to China if Russia appeared on the verge of terminating military shipments. (Arab apologists, while continuing to insist that their case is a purely moral one, at the same time argue that the United States should turn against Israel on the purely expediential grounds that the intrusion of Sino-Soviet rivalry in the region will guarantee us a whole series of Middle Eastern Viet Nams if we don't.)

Some outside power or powers could impose a settlement by coercion in one form or another. As already noted in Chapter 5, this kind of solution would inevitably be resented, and probably would be very temporary.

The outside powers have attempted to use their good offices in an off-again-on-again effort to bring the two sides together. The United States has perhaps the most admirable record in this regard, offering to underwrite a number of joint development projects that would benefit both Israel and the Arab states. These have ranged from an ambitious scheme to generate hydroelectric power by dropping Mediterranean water 1,290 feet through tunnels to the Dead Sea to development of Jordan River water resources and the desalinization of seawater.

But none of the outside powers has consistently given its best efforts to resolving the Middle East crisis either severally or jointly, inside or outside the UN framework. If the outside powers and parties gave strong and consistent evidence of an enthusiastic commitment to Middle Eastern peace through energetic diplomatic activity, clear indication that they did not propose to support belligerence (even short of an arms embargo), and a credible undertaking to support and underwrite a negotiated settlement by political, military, and economic means, they might influence the situation in a constructive direction. Outside encouragement may help to get the contenders to the table and keep them there. Outside suggestions may point the way to a viable settlement. But no adequate substitute for a peace treaty negotiated by the parties to the dispute has yet been devised.

Ultimately, a willingness on the part of Arab leaders to come to a nonviolent settlement with Israel and to promote it among their own people with the same energy that they have devoted to the cause of violent solution offers the most viable if not the only means to a resolution of the crisis. To some extent Arab leaders may have painted themselves into a corner with slow-drying enamel by their reiterated anti-Israel propaganda. They might find a graceful way out difficult to achieve, even if they wanted one. Pretty clearly they have created a Frankenstein monster through their patronage of the Arab guerrilla movement, one that threatens to usurp their own place in the halls of power. But is it unreasonable to hope the Arab people are not cursed with a capacity for undying hatred? One may suspect that hatred of Israel is not so deep and universal as the official Arab position holds, that the generosity and civility that characterize private Arab transactions are also capable of expression in public policy. Surely it is not insane to suppose that the peoples of the Arab world would accept a fair and just negotiated settlement with Israel if it were presented to them frankly. But first many would have to be prepared for the very idea that negotiation is desirable, since the contrary notion has been drummed home so relentlessly for so long. Arab leaders sometimes act as if they held their own people in contempt. In an action of such far-reaching consequences they would need to take their people into their confidence.

What are the chances for such a radical shift in public Arab policy? On the record of the past half century one cannot be very optimistic. Many Israelis believe that a line has formed of nations eager to be the second Arab state to sign a peace treaty with Israel. Even if the wish is not the father to the thought in this instance, the courageous first signer must be located and must have sufficient prestige and survival power to open the way for the next and the next and the next. One cannot lodge much hope in the rise of a new generation of more moderate leaders. Younger Arabs may be even more polarized than their elders vis-à-vis Israel. There is as yet little evidence that the youthful demand for peace that is finding expression in America and Europe (on both sides of the Iron Curtain, to the consternation of the Eastern-bloc bureaucracy) has penetrated Arab youth organizations. Nevertheless, this kind of change is the one best hope for peace in the Middle East, and possibly in the world.

125. Prospects for the future

It may be premature to speculate about the outcome of a peace conference that is as yet not even a lively prospect. It is impossible to anticipate the details of any agreement that free Arab-Israeli negotiation could produce. But surely it is useful to point out that a fair and just settlement is possible, and to suggest a general shape it might take. Obviously it would involve Arab recognition of Israel as a legitimate sovereign state. An attempt to reach behind May 15, 1948, would only scuttle negotiations before they began. The Arab states could quite legitimately adopt the bargaining position that Israel's legal boundaries had been defined by the UN partition resolution of November 29, 1947. Israel holds that the openly avowed Arab aggression of 1948, directed as much against the UN partition as against Israel herself, rendered the 1947 territorial allocations a dead issue. Israel would enter the conference with the territories occupied in 1967 as bargaining counters, but would probably regard the 1949 armistice lines as the real borders, to be redrawn with some adjustments into secure and recognized boundaries. In other words, Israel would give up the gains of 1967 in return for peace. A significant concession that the Arabs could grant Israel would be demilitarization of the West Bank and the Sinai peninsula. The concession would not be so large as it might sound. It would recognize the geographic fact that the Jordan Valley is Israel's eastern strategic frontier, that her Negev territories have no well-defined natural defense line, and that apart from the feud with Israel, Egypt has no strategic need for a fortified Sharm el Sheikh (unless she is planning a war against Jordan). An Arab move of this sort would remove any reason for an Israeli demand for territorial concessions to provide the essential strategic buffer. Israel's limited territory would prevent her from establishing a corresponding neutral zone on her own borders, though she might undertake to keep heavy military equipment back a certain distance and eschew offensive installations in border zones.

The demilitarization line in Sinai could be drawn far enough north to enable Egypt to provide full security for both banks of the Suez Canal. Both sides would be permitted to deploy light constabulary forces right up to the national borders or to the edge of a narrow buffer zone along the demarcation line. This would be essential to permit control of dissident elements disgruntled by the peace settlement, and to prevent other types of brigandage and illegal border crossing.

Israel would pay a much larger price for this kind of solution than meets the eye. Just as one example, her pre-1967 borders do not provide enough space for the strategic dispersal of aircraft against surprise attack, a luxury provided by the 1967 occupation. Similar demilitarization could be applied in the Galilee–Golan Heights sector. The most powerful strategic consideration would oblige Israel to continue her occupation of the Golan area should this not be accomplished. Syria has been the most adamant of the Arab states in her official refusal to negotiate with Israel. Should this position be maintained in the face of a more moderate stance by her co-belligerents, the other Arab states would simply have to recognize that Israel has no other viable strategic choice in that area.

Elsewhere, minor territorial adjustments could be mutually desirable. Doubtless Israel would like to be relieved of the Latrun salient, which blocked the direct Tel Aviv–Jerusalem highway and positioned Arab forces within fifteen miles of the sea at her vulnerable middle, within easy artillery shot of Tel Aviv and Lod Airport.

Jerusalem constitutes the most vexing territorial problem and hence requires more elaborate discussion. Both ordinary Israelis and their leaders regard the 1967 occupation of all Jerusalem not as a conquest but as the liberation and re-unification of Israel's historic capital, her most sacred place, and the seat of her ancient glories.

It would be incorrect to say that Israel is adamant on the subject of Jerusalem, despite the fact that Israel's parliament has solidified the reunification of the city by legislation. Mrs. Meir indicated, on the NBC television program "Meet the Press" of September 28, 1969, that the topic of Jerusalem would not be taboo in any future negotiations with the Arab states. Israel would hardly allow even so important an issue

President Nixon welcomes Golda Meir, Israel's Prime Minister, on White House grounds, 1969.

as Jerusalem to block a settlement provided there was genuine agreement from the Arab side to reasonable and meaningful resolution of all other issues. The irony that would come if the City of Peace prolonged a state of war is not lost on Israel. Nor are Israelis less aware than other persons that Jerusalem has come to symbolize revelations of God to mankind and aspirations of the human spirit which transcend every particularity, precisely because of Israel's evocative historical involvement with the place. In other words, if David has located his capital and Solomon had built his temple at Shechem of Jericho, Jerusalem would be no more controversial than Ramalla. To say that Jerusalem is sacred to three religions is a cliché that points inadequately to this truth.

But Jerusalem is sacred to Judaism in a much stronger sense than it is to Islam or to most contemporary forms of Christianity. One simply cannot underestimate the significance that the holy places of Jerusalem bear for Jews, and especially for Israeli Jews. Rabbi Abraham Heschel's *Israel, an Echo of Eternity,* which approaches the poetic transport of Judah ha-Levi, is required reading for anyone who would understand the powerful organic attachment between Judaism and the Holy Land, above all Jerusalem. The operative question in connection with Jerusalem may be: "How far could an Israeli government compromise its position on Jerusalem and still remain a government?"

Compromise is the key word. Mutually acceptable compromise is the alternative to imposition when a matter is contended. The Arab governments would also be obliged to strive for a formula that would accommodate the legitimate concerns of their own people. The interests and desires of other concerned bystanders, such as the international religious communities and the Arabs of east Jerusalem (whose best interests do not necessarily coincide with those of the external Arab states), also deserve consideration.

Jerusalem was a single metropolitan area prior to the events of 1947–49. Quite aside from all other factors, Jerusalem would be most practically administered as a single unit. However, the divisions wrought by chance and history are sufficiently visible to play an inevitable part in discussions of the city's future. It may be useful to review them.

The new sector of West Jerusalem, first settled in 1856, developed when the Jewish population overflowed the limited area of the Jewish Quarter in the old walled city. (See map on pages 130–31.) Largely Jewish before 1948 and Israeli territory since, this is Israel's capital. The Mount Scopus enclave encompassed major Jewish educational and humanitarian institutions—Hadassah Hospital, the Hebrew University, and the National Library. Israel managed to hold

Sixteenth-century walls built by Suleiman the Magnificent enclose the Old City of Jerusalem.

it through the 1948 war, but it remained isolated in the midst of territory held by Jordan from 1948 to 1967.

The new area of East Jerusalem, predominantly Arab, was also the site of many European religious and educational institutions and a sizable Jewish population in the Sheikh Jerrah Quarter. Prior to 1948, Israelis had both tangible and sentimental interest in East Jerusalem, including the ancient Mount of Olives cemetery, which was desecrated during the Jordanian occupation.

The walled Old City, containing the principal Jewish, Christian, and Moslem holy places and the historic Jewish Quarter (overrun during the 1948 war but now in the process of restoration), is the major bone of contention.

It is absolutely certain that Israel will never willingly return to the situation that obtained from 1948 to 1967. Israel will not hand East Jerusalem, particularly the Old City, back

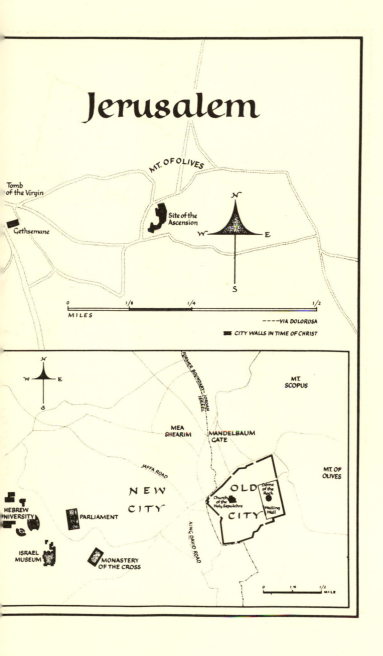

Jerusalem

MT. OF OLIVES

Tomb
of the Virgin

Site of the
Ascension

N

Gethsemane

W   E

S

MILES
0   1/8   1/4   1/2

- - - - VIA DOLOROSA

CITY WALLS IN TIME OF CHRIST

N

W   E

S

MT.
SCOPUS

FORMER BOUNDARY
JORDAN — ISRAEL

MEA
SHEARIM

MANDELBAUM
GATE

JAFFA ROAD

MT. OF
OLIVES

NEW
CITY

OLD
Dome of the
Rock

Church of the
Holy Sepulchre

HEBREW
UNIVERSITY

PARLIAMENT

CITY

Wailing
Wall

KING DAVID ROAD

ISRAEL
MUSEUM

MONASTERY
OF THE CROSS

0   1/4   1/2
MILE

to Jordan, which annexed it by force in violation of the UN partition plan of 1947 and barred Jewish pilgrims from its holy places in violation of both the 1947 plan and the 1949 armistice accords. Publicly this is the only solution that has been advocated from the Arab side. It is to be hoped it is not the only solution the Arab nations would entertain at a peace conference.

A continuation of the status quo in Jerusalem would, of course, be quite congenial to many in Israel. It is dubious that any Arab government would affix its signature to a treaty that would explicitly embody such terms. The most readily foreseeable circumstance leading to this outcome would be one in which there was no peace treaty but a marathon extension of the present crisis, or a simmering down of the crisis with the Arabs accommodating them‑ selves to the fact of a united Israeli Jerusalem. Israel's grudging acceptance of the Jordanian *fait accompli*—until Jordan's entry into the 1967 war provided the occasion to change things—provides a precedent.

It is most likely, however, that the final agreement on Jerusalem will be a compromise encompassing elements of various proposals already advanced and, most important, the product of imaginative negotiation.

The problems of Jerusalem should not be insoluble in the face of the mutual will to solve them. Neither side has yet produced a packet of clearly enunciated compromise pro‑ posals on Jerusalem. That both Arab and Israeli statesmen as well as intellectuals outside government are capable of solving this difficult and sensitive problem should not be doubted. Indeed, all of the problems of the Middle East are capable of solution. Abba Eban commented before the UN General Assembly on September 19, 1969, that "Israel is pre‑ pared to negotiate without prior conditions of any kind."

The final disposition of the West Bank lands ought to take into account the desires of the people of the area. They might possibly become a part of Jordan or an independent Palestinian Arab state involved in any of a variety of com‑ mercial and security arrangements. It is possible that Israel would grant port facilities at Haifa and one of her more

Marketing in the Arab town of Nablus, on the West Bank.

southerly Mediterranean ports to the Palestinians and Jordanians along with overland transport rights. Among the mutual benefits that could accrue from peace would be the inauguration of peaceful rail transit through Israel to various points in the Arab world and highway travel rights for Israel through the West Bank. Freedom of navigation on international waterways could be guaranteed. With the passage of time, normal commercial relations should develop. Israel has pointed out many times how her reservoir of technical skills could be of immeasurable benefit to the region. Israel and Lebanon together are ideally situated to play a role in their region not unlike that of Switzerland in Europe. One gathers that both are quite ready to assume that role as soon as external and internal conditions permit.

Guilty and innocent alike are in line for an indeterminate share of the unpleasant practical consequences of delay in working out a solution. Time grows shorter, and we never had too much to begin with. It isn't an exercise in pessimism to observe that Middle Eastern political and diplomatic relationships—already bad enough—have deteriorated since late 1967. The eruption of actual armed conflict between the Arab guerrilla organizations and the relatively moderate government of Lebanon in the autumn of 1969 marked not a new departure but merely a new nadir in a well-advanced process. If the unraveling of the fabric of life in the Middle East has done no more than fray the edges of world relationships to this point, that is small comfort. It may have done more than this already. As it continues, the damage promises to be progressive and cumulative. There is a temptation to assert that it is going to be a long decade in the Middle East if we don't find a solution, or at least start heading toward one.

But then a second thought arises: It may not be a long decade after all. Maybe not even a decade. The match is to the fuse, and not all the world's powder is stored in a distant corner of the Mediterranean.

Appendices

1. Chronology

Landmarks of 4,000 years of Jewish life in Israel

I. The Biblical Period

18th to 16th centuries B.C.	The Patriarchs: Abraham, Isaac, and Jacob.
15th to 14th centuries	Moses: Exodus from Egypt; conquest of Canaan.
13th to 11th centuries	Judges: Deborah, Gideon, Samson.
Mid-11th to mid-10th centuries	Kings: Saul, David, Solomon.

c. 1000	David makes Jerusalem the capital.
c. 960	Solomon builds the Temple there.
c. 930	Kingdom divided into Judea and Northern Kingdom (Israel).
721	Conquest of Northern Kingdom by Assyrians.
586	Conquest of Judea by Babylonians and destruction of Jerusalem.
538–515	First return from captivity in Babylon. Rebuilding of the Temple.

II. Second Temple Period: 515 B.C. to 70 A.D.

457–424	Second Babylonian return. Ezra and Nehemiah.
333	Conquest by Alexander the Great.
323–168	Rule by Hellenist successors to Alexander.
168–165	Revolt of the Maccabees. Beginning of the Hasmonean dynasty.
63	Beginning of Roman rule.
37	End of Hasmonean dynasty.
37–34 A.D.	King Herod.
66–70	Revolt against Rome.
70	Destruction of the Second Temple by Romans. Only Western Wall remains.
73	Last stand of the rebels at Masada.

III. Alien Suzerainty

132–135	Bar-Kochba's uprising against Rome.
c. 200	Completion of Mishna (codification of Jewish Law).
352	Jewish uprising against Rome in Galilee.
395–638	Byzantine rule.
c. 400	Completion of Jerusalem Talmud.
614	Persian invasion, supported by Jewish army.

636	Beginning of Arab rule.
700–900	Masoretic text of the Bible determined.
1072	Conquest by Seljuk Turks.
1099	Crusaders take Jerusalem and massacre the Jews of the city, destroy other Jewish settlements.
1141	Spanish poet Judah Halevi's journey to Holy Land spurs new wave of immigration from France, England, Spain, and Germany.
1267	Nachmanides visits Jerusalem and revives its Jewish community.
1291	End of Crusader rule, Mameluke Conquest.
1350	Migrations from Germany and Italy.
1492	Jews expelled from Spain, many migrate to Holy Land.
1500	Safed becomes spiritual center.
1577	First Jewish printing press in country.
1750's	Hasidic migration from Poland, Russia, and Galicia.
1799	Napoleonic invasion.
1856	First Jewish quarter outside the walled city of Jerusalem.
1870	Agricultural school founded in Mikve Israel.
1878	Petach Tikva, first pioneering village founded.
1882	First Aliyah, modern wave of immigration, begins; new villages founded.
1895	Theodor Herzl writes *The Jewish State*.
1897	First Zionist Congress in Basel calls for "establishing for the Jewish people a publicly and legally assured home in Palestine."
1901	Jewish land-purchasing agency formed (Jewish National Fund).
1904–1914	Second Aliyah.
1907	Jewish population in Palestine is 80,000.
1909	Tel Aviv, first all-Jewish city, founded.
1911	Degania, first *kvutza* (collective village) founded.
1917	Balfour Declaration. Cornerstone of Hebrew University laid in Jerusalem.

1917–1918 British military occupation.

1920 Third Aliyah begins. Histaudrut (General Federation of Jewish Labor) founded. Haganah, Jewish underground self-defense organization, formed.

1921 Nahalal, first *moshav* (cooperative smallholders' village) founded.

1922 Arab outbreaks. British Mandate over Palestine and Transjordan confirmed by League of Nations.

Transjordan detached by British Government and set up as independent kingdom.

1925 Hebrew University opened on Mount Scopus.

1929 Arab riots—Jewish community of Hebron massacred.

1935–1947 Nazi Holocaust Era.

1935 Fifth Aliyah—Exodus of German Jewry—61,854 new immigrants enter.

1936 Arab riots in Jaffa, led by Mufti.

1937 Royal Commission, headed by Lord Peel, recognizes historic bond between the Jewish people and its Land, proposes partition plan.

1938–1939 Massive arrivals of "illegal" immigrants, totalling 115,000.

1939 New White Paper on Palestine issued by Chamberlain Government, stating that no further Jewish immigration would be allowed after another 75,000 had come in. Limits land purchase.

First Jewish units join the British to fight Hitler.

1944 Jewish Brigade formed as separate Jewish fighting force of the British Army.

1945 British Prime Minister Bevin advocates placing Israel under international trusteeship—British occupation without the Mandate and its obligations.

1946 Anglo-American Committee recommends immediate admission of 100,000 Jewish displaced persons; Atlee refuses. Illegal immigration increases and the Palestine Jewish community organizes for resistance.

Arab sabotage.

1947   British Government submits problem to UN.

Ben Gurion appears before General Assembly.
USSR supports Jewish claims. General Assembly establishes the United Nations Special Committee on Palestine (UNSCOP).

UNSCOP recommends termination of British Mandate, independence for Palestine "as soon as possible," the shortest possible transition period, and UN responsibility for administration during transition. Majority of Committee proposes partition with Jerusalem as separate body under international administrator.

UN General Assembly votes acceptance of majority report by 33 to 13, and 10 abstentions (including Britain). British maintain occupying army of 75,000 to 100,000.

Arabs launch assault. Hagana mobilized.
British stand by.

Beginning of Arab exodus from area allotted to Jewish state.

1948   Birth of the State of Israel (May 14). End of British Mandate.

Invasion of Israel by armies of Egypt, Lebanon, Syria, Iraq, and Transjordan.

U.S. recognizes new state *de facto* (*de jure* recognition given in 1949). Israel recognized *de jure* by Soviet Union, followed by thirteen other countries.

Large-scale immigration begins.

Jews in Old City of Jerusalem surrender to Arab Legion.

UN Security Council requests for truces accepted.

UN emissary Count Bernadotte murdered in Jerusalem.

Dissident underground organizations (Irgun and Stern Gang) give up arms and join Israel Defense Forces.

Security Council asks Israel and Egypt to open peace negotiations. Egypt does not comply. Fighting continues and Israel gains possession of Negev.

1949	End of fighting. Negotiations begin in Rhodes with assistance of Dr. Ralph Bunche, UN Assistant Secretary General.
	First Knesset (Parliament) elects Weizmann President.
	Armistice Agreement (with Egypt) signed.
	Israel occupies Eilat, on Gulf of Aqaba.
	Ben Gurion forms first regular government.
	Israel becomes member of UN.
	UN Assembly votes complete internationalization of Jerusalem. Arab states and Israel oppose Knesset transfer of Jerusalem.
1950	Knesset passes Law of the Return, confirming right of every Jew to dwell in Israel.
1951	Massive immigration doubles Israel's population between 1948 and 1951. 850,000 acres under cultivation. Immigrants from Germany and DP camps followed by entire communities from Yemen, Iraq, and remnants of Polish Jewry.
	Adenauer agrees to reparations from Germany.
	Security Council confirms Israel's right to freedom of navigation in Suez Canal, condemns Egypt's anti-Israel blockade.
1952	Death of Chaim Weizmann. Yitzhak Ben Zvi succeeds him as President.
1953	First Prime Minister David Ben Gurion retires to Sde Boker, kibbutz in the Negev.
1954	Moshe Sharett becomes Premier.
	Security Council resolution calling on Egypt to lift Suez Canal blockage vetoed by USSR.
	Hebrew University dedicates new campus in Jerusalem.
1955	Egyptian-Czech arms deal announced.
	Ben Gurion recalled to form new government; offers to discuss settlement with Arabs in view of renewed threats from Cairo. Arab terrorist attacks account for 884 Israeli casualties between 1950 and 1955. Attacks from Gaza Strip and Sinai multiply.

141. Appendices

1956   Israel warns UN to enforce cease fire or Israel will defend its own citizens. Attacks continue.

Egypt, Jordan, and Syria sign military alliance. Israel mobilizes reserves.

Israeli forces attack Sinai, clear it of Egyptian guerrilla bases and regular troop concentrations. Take Gaza Strip and Sharm el-Sheikh. Suez crisis.

Israel complies with UN cease fire. UN demands immediate evacuation of British and French forces from Egyptian territory and withdrawal of Israeli troops to behind 1949 Armistice lines. Israel agrees to withdraw forces "upon conclusion of satisfactory arrangements with the UN . . ."

1957   UN Emergency Force stationed in Sinai and Gaza Strip.

Israel evacuates Sinai and Gaza Strip on receiving assurances of free passage in Tiran Straits. Freedom of navigation in the Red Sea ensues.

First ship reaches Eilat port.

1958   Opening of Beersheba-Eilat highway—Israel's "dry land Suez Canal."

1961   Eichmann trial, followed by his execution in 1962.

Millionth immigrant since establishment of state.

1963   President Ben Zvi dies. Zalman Shazar elected Israel's third President.

Prime Minister Ben Gurion resigns. Levi Eshkol becomes Prime Minister.

1964   Pope Paul VI visits Christian holy sites in Israel.

1965   Israel and West Germany agree to establish diplomatic relations.

1966   Israel calls on UN to halt Syrian border aggression.

New Knesset building opened in Jerusalem.

Abba Eban presents Israel's case against Syrian aggression to Security Council.

Military Government in border areas abolished.

S. Y. Agnon receives Nobel Prize for Literature.

1967   Syrians bring about deadlock in discussions on border problems.

Nasser moves massive armor into Sinai as Israel celebrates 19th Independence Day.

U Thant rebuts allegations of Israeli troop concentrations near Syrian frontier; UN Emergency Force in Sinai and Gaza Strip withdrawn at Nasser's demand.

Nasser declares Tiran Straits closed to Israeli shipping and cargoes; announces readiness for "all-out" war.

Hussein of Jordan signs anti-Israel pact with Egypt, placing his forces under Egyptian command.

Iraqi and Saudi Arabian troops enter Jordan.

Iraq signs anti-Israel pact with Egypt.

Egypt moves Sinai armor toward Israel. Israel destroys Egyptian airpower. Jordan and Syria join in assault on Israel. Israel forces advance into Sinai, occupy Gaza Strip; clear Jordanian offensive out of Jerusalem and areas west of River Jordan, reach Suez Canal, storm Syrian fortifications on Golan Heights.

Jerusalem reunified.

UN Security Council resolution calls for Middle East settlement and withdrawal of forces.

1968   Repeated incursions by terrorists along Jordan and Syrian borders, Suez, and Gaza Strip; Israeli forces respond.

Complete replenishment of Egyptian military materiel by USSR.

Constant artillery barrage across Suez Canal.

Foreign Minister Abba Eban presents nine-point plan to UN General Assembly.

New Arabic newspapers published in Jerusalem.

William Scranton, President-elect Nixon's special envoy to Middle East, visits Israel.

Arab terrorists attack El-Al plane in Athens. One passenger killed.

U.S. promises to supply fifty Phantom jets to Israel.

Israel stages retaliatory raid on Beirut Airport.

1969   Terrorist activities continue on the Galilee, Jordanian,
Lebanese, and Syrian borders, in occupied territory,
and in Jerusalem and Tel Aviv.

France places embargo on all military supplies to
Israel; refuses to refund monies paid for them.

Iraq hangs fourteen as Israeli spies.

Levi Eshkol dies. Golda Meir becomes Israel's fourth
Prime Minister.

Al Aksa Mosque set on fire.

Abba Eban speaks before the United Nations, says
everything is negotiable.

Golda Meir visits the United States.

2. Documents

The Balfour Declaration

November 2nd, 1917.
Foreign Office

Dear Lord Rothschild,

I have much pleasure in conveying to you, on behalf of His
Majesty's Government, the following declaration of sympathy with
Jewish Zionist aspirations which has been submitted to, and ap-
proved by, the Cabinet.

"His Majesty's Government view with favour the establishment
in Palestine of a national home for the Jewish people, and will use
their best endeavours to facilitate the achievement of this object, it
being clearly understood that nothing shall be done which may
prejudice the civil and religious rights of existing non-Jewish communities in Palestine, or the rights and political status enjoyed by
Jews in any other country."

I should be grateful if you would bring this declaration to the
knowledge of the Zionist Federation.

Yours sincerely,
ARTHUR JAMES BALFOUR

U.N. General Assembly Resolution on the Future Government of Palestine (Partition Plan)

November 29, 1947

The General Assembly,

Having met in special session at the request of the mandatory Power to constitute and instruct a special committee to prepare for the consideration of the question of the future government of Palestine at the second regular session;

Having constituted a Special Committee and instructed it to investigate all questions and issues relevant to the problem of Palestine, and to prepare proposals for the solution of the problem, and

Having received and examined the report of the Special Committee (document A/364) including a number of unanimous recommendations and a plan of partition with economic union approved by the majority of the Special Committee,

Considers that the present situation in Palestine is one which is likely to impair the general welfare and friendly relations among nations;

Takes note of the declaration by the mandatory Power that it plans to complete its evacuation of Palestine by 1 August 1948;

Recommends to the United Kingdom, as the mandatory Power for Palestine, and to all other Members of the United Nations the adoption and implementation, with regard to the future government of Palestine, of the Plan of Partition with Economic Union set out below;

Requests that

(a) The Security Council take the necessary measures as provided for in the plan for its implementation;

(b) The Security Council consider, if circumstances during the transitional period require such consideration, whether the situation in Palestine constitutes a threat to the peace. If it decides that such a threat exists, and in order to maintain international peace and security, the Security Council should supplement the authorization of the General Assembly by taking measures, under Article 39 and 41 of the Charter, to empower the United Nations Commission, as provided in this resolution, to exercise in Palestine the functions which are assigned to it by this resolution;

(c) The Security Council determine as a threat to the peace, breach of the peace or act of aggression, in accordance with Article 39 of the Charter, any attempt to alter by force the settlement envisaged by this resolution;

(d) The Trusteeship Council be informed of the responsibilities envisaged for it in this plan;

Calls upon the inhabitants of Palestine to take such steps as may be necessary on their part to put this plan into effect;

Appeals to all Governments and all peoples to refrain from taking any action which might hamper or delay the carrying out of these recommendations, and

Authorizes the Secretary-General to reimburse travel and subsistence expenses of the members of the Commission referred to in Part I, Section B, paragraph 1 below, on such basis and in such form as he may determine most appropriate in the circumstances, and to provide the Commission with the necessary staff to assist in carrying out the functions assigned to the Commission by the General Assembly.

Plan of Partition with Economic Union, Part I
Future Constitution and Government of Palestine*

A. TERMINATION OF MANDATE PARTITION AND INDEPENDENCE

1. The Mandate for Palestine shall terminate as soon as possible but in any case not later than 1 August 1948.

2. The armed forces of the mandatory Power shall be progressively withdrawn from Palestine, the withdrawal to be completed as soon as possible but in any case not later than 1 August 1948.

The mandatory Power shall advise the Commission, as far in advance as possible, of its intention to terminate the Mandate and to evacuate each area.

The mandatory Power shall use its best endeavours to ensure that an area situated in the territory of the Jewish State, including a seaport and hinterland adequate to provide facilities for a substantial immigration, shall be evacuated at the earliest possible date and in any event not later than 1 February 1948.

3. Independent Arab and Jewish States and the Special International Regime for the City of Jerusalem, set forth in part III of this plan, shall come into existence in Palestine two months after the evacuation of the armed forces of the mandatory Power has been completed but in any case not later than 1 October 1948. The

*Not included here are Part I, Section D, Part II and Part III.

boundaries of the Arab State, the Jewish State, and the City of Jerusalem shall be described in parts II and III below.

4. The period between the adoption by the General Assembly of its recommendation on the question of Palestine and the establishment of the independence of the Arab and Jewish States shall be a transitional period.

B. STEPS PREPARATORY TO INDEPENDENCE

1. A Commission shall be set up consisting of one representative of each of the five Member States. The Members represented on the Commission shall be elected by the General Assembly on as broad a basis, geographically and otherwise, as possible.

2. The administration of Palestine shall, as the mandatory Power withdraws its armed forces, be progressively turned over to the Commission, which shall act in conformity with the recommendations of the General Assembly, under the guidance of the Security Council. The mandatory Power shall to the fullest possible extent co-ordinate its plans for withdrawal with the plans of the Commission to take over and administer areas which have been evacuated.

In the discharge of this administrative responsibility the Commission shall have authority to issue necessary regulations and take other measures as required.

The mandatory Power shall not take any action to prevent, obstruct or delay the implementation by the Commission of the measures recommended by the General Assembly.

3. On its arrival in Palestine the Commission shall proceed to carry out measures for the establishment of the frontiers of the Arab and Jewish States and the City of Jerusalem in accordance with the general lines of the recommendations of the General Assembly on the partition of Palestine. Nevertheless, the boundaries as described in part II of this plan are to be modified in such a way that village areas as a rule will not be divided by state boundaries unless pressing reasons make that necessary.

4. The Commission, after consultation with the democratic parties and other public organizations of the Arab and Jewish States, shall select and establish in each State as rapidly as possible a Provisional Council of Government. The activities of both the Arab and Jewish Provisional Councils of Government shall be carried out under the general direction of the Commission.

If by 1 April 1948 a Provisional Council of Government cannot be selected for either of the States, or, if selected, cannot carry out its functions, the Commissions shall communicate that fact to the

Security Council for such action with respect to that State as the Security Council may deem proper, and to the Secretary-General for communication to the Members of the United Nations.

5. Subject to the provisions of these recommendations, during the transitional period the Provisional Councils of Government, acting under the Commission, shall have full authority in the areas under their control, including authority over matters of immigration and land regulation.

6. The Provisional Council of Government of each State, acting under the Commission, shall progressively receive from the Commission full responsibility for the administration of that State in the period between the termination of the Mandate and the establishment of the State's independence.

7. The Commission shall instruct the Provisional Councils of Government of both the Arab and Jewish States, after their formation, to proceed to the establishment of administrative organs of government, central and local.

8. The Provisional Council of Government of each State shall, within the shortest time possible, recruit an armed militia from the residents of that State, sufficient in number to maintain internal order and to prevent frontier clashes.

This armed militia in each State shall, for operational purposes, be under the command of Jewish or Arab officers resident in that State, but general political and military control, including the choice of the militia's High Command, shall be exercised by the Commission.

9. The Provisional Council of Government of each State shall, not later than two months after the withdrawal of the armed forces of the mandatory Power, hold elections to the Constituent Assembly which shall be conducted on democratic lines.

The election regulations in each State shall be drawn up by the Provisional Council of Government and approved by the Commission.

Qualified voters for each State for this election shall be persons over eighteen years of age who are: (a) Palestinian citizens residing in that State and (b) Arabs and Jews residing in the State, although not Palestinian citizens, who, before voting, have signed a notice of intention to become citizens of such State.

Arabs and Jews residing in the City of Jerusalem who have signed a notice of intention to become citizens, the Arabs of the Arab State and the Jews of the Jewish State, shall be entitled to vote in the Arab and Jewish States respectively.

Women may vote and be elected to the Constituent Assemblies.

During the transitional period no Jew shall be permitted to establish residence in the area of the proposed Arab State, and no Arab shall be permitted to establish residence in the area of the proposed Jewish State, except by special leave of the Commission.

10. The Constituent Assembly of each State shall draft a democratic constitution for its State and choose a provisional government to succeed the Provisional Council of Government appointed by the Commission. The constitutions of the States shall embody chapters 1 and 2 of the Declaration provided for in section C below and include *inter alia* provisions for:

(a) Establishing in each State a legislative body elected by universal suffrage and by secret ballot on the basis of proportional representation, and an executive body responsible to the legislature;

(b) Settling all international disputes in which the State may be involved by peaceful means in such a manner that international peace and security, and justice, are not endangered;

(c) Accepting the obligation of the State to refrain in its international relations from the threat or use of force against the territorial integrity or political independence of any State, or in any other manner inconsistent with the purposes of the United Nations;

(d) Guaranteeing to all persons equal and non-discriminatory rights in civil, political, economic and religious matters, and the enjoyment of human rights and fundamental freedoms, including freedom of religion, language, speech and publication, education, assembly and association;

(e) Preserving freedom of transit and visit for all residents and citizens of the other State in Palestine and the City of Jerusalem, subject to considerations of national security, provided that each State shall control residence within its borders.

11. The Commission shall appoint a preparatory economic commission of three members to make whatever arrangements are possible for economic co-operation, with a view to establishing, as soon as practicable, the Economic Union and the Joint Economic Board, as provided in section D below.

12. During the period between the adoption of the recommendations on the question of Palestine by the General Assembly and the termination of the Mandate, the mandatory Power in Palestine shall maintain full responsibility for administration in areas from which it has not withdrawn its armed forces. The Commission shall assist the mandatory Power in the carrying out of these functions. Simi-

larly the mandatory Power shall co-operate with the Commission in the execution of its functions.

13. With a view to ensuring that there shall be continuity in the functioning of administrative services and that, on the withdrawal of the armed forces of the mandatory Power, the whole administration shall be in charge of the Provisional Councils and the Joint Economic Board, respectively, acting under the Commission, there shall be a progressive transfer, from the mandatory Power to the Commission, of responsibility for all the functions of government, including that of maintaining law and order in the areas from which the forces of the mandatory Power have been withdrawn.

14. The Commission shall be guided in its activities by the recommendations of the General Assembly and by such instructions as the Security Council may consider necessary to issue.

The measures taken by the Commission, within the recommendations of the General Assembly, shall become immediately effective unless the Commission has previously received contrary instructions from the Security Council.

The Commission shall render periodic monthly progress reports, or more frequently if desirable, to the Security Council.

15. The Commission shall make its final report to the next regular session of the General Assembly and to the Security Council simultaneously.

C. DECLARATION

A declaration shall be made to the United Nations by the provisional government of each proposed State before independence. It shall contain *inter alia* the following clauses:

General Provision

The stipulations contained in the declaration are recognized as fundamental laws of the State and no law, regulation or official action shall conflict or interfere with these stipulations, nor shall any law, regulation or official action prevail over them.

Chapter 1. Holy Places, Religious Buildings and Sites

1. Existing rights in respect of Holy Places and religious buildings or sites shall not be denied or impaired.

2. In so far as Holy Places are concerned, the liberty of access, visit and transit shall be guaranteed, in conformity with existing rights, to all residents and citizens of the other State and of the City

of Jerusalem, as well as to aliens, without distinction as to nationality, subject to requirements of national security, public order and decorum.

Similarly, freedom of worship shall be guaranteed in conformity with existing rights, subject to the maintenance of public order and decorum.

3. Holy Places and religious buildings or sites shall be preserved. No act shall be permitted which may in any way impair their sacred character. If at any time it appears to the Government that any particular Holy Place, religious building or site is in need of urgent repair, the Government may call upon the community or communities concerned to carry out such repair. The Government may carry it out itself at the expense of the community or communities concerned if no action is taken within a reasonable time.

4. No taxation shall be levied in respect of any Holy Place, religious building or site which was exempt from taxation on the date of the creation of the State.

No change in the incidence of such taxation shall be made which would either discriminate between the owners or occupiers of Holy Places, religious buildings or sites, or would place such owners or occupiers in a position less favourable in relation to the general incidence of taxation than existed at the time of the adoption of the Assembly's recommendation.

5. The Governor of the City of Jerusalem shall have the right to determine whether the provisions of the Constitution of the State in relation to Holy Places, religious buildings and sites within the borders of the State and the religious rights appertaining thereto, are being properly applied and respected, and to make decisions on the basis of existing rights in cases of disputes which may arise between the different religious communities or the rites of a religious community with respect to such places, buildings and sites. He shall receive full co-operation and such privileges and immunities as are necessary for the exercise of his functions in the State.

Chapter 2. Religious and Minority Rights

1. Freedom of conscience and the free exercise of all forms of worship, subject only to the maintenance of public order and morals, shall be ensured to all.

2. No discrimination of any kind shall be made between the inhabitants on the ground of race, religion, language or sex.

3. All persons within the jurisdiction of the State shall be entitled to equal protection of the laws.

4. The family law and personal status of the various minorities and their religious interests, including endowments, shall be respected.

5. Except as may be required for the maintenance of public order and good government, no measure shall be taken to obstruct or interfere with the enterprise of religious or charitable bodies of all faiths or to discriminate against any representative or member of these bodies on the ground of his religion or nationality.

6. The State shall ensure adequate primary and secondary education for the Arab and Jewish minority, respectively, in its own language and its cultural traditions.

The right of each community to maintain its own schools for the education of its own members in its own language, while conforming to such educational requirements of a general nature as the State may impose, shall not be denied or impaired. Foreign educational establishments shall continue their activity on the basis of their existing rights.

7. No restriction shall be imposed on the free use by any citizen of the State of any language in private intercourse, in commerce, in religion, in the Press or in publications of any kind, or at public meetings.[1]

8. No expropriation of land owned by an Arab in the Jewish State (by a Jew in the Arab State)[2] shall be allowed except for public purposes. In all cases of expropriation full compensation as fixed by the Supreme Court shall be paid previous to dispossession.

Chapter 3. Citizenship, International Conventions and Financial Obligations

1. *Citizenship.* Palestinian citizens residing in Palestine outside the City of Jerusalem, as well as Arabs and Jews who, not holding Palestinian citizenship, reside in Palestine outside the City of Jerusalem shall, upon the recognition of independence, become citizens of the State in which they are resident and enjoy full civil and political rights. Persons over the age of eighteen years may opt, within one year from the date of recognition of independence of the State in which they reside, for citizenship of the other State, provid-

1. The following stipulation shall be added to the declaration concerning the Jewish State: "In the Jewish State adequate facilities shall be given to Arabic-speaking citizens for the use of their language, either orally or in writing, in the legislature, before the Courts and in the administration."

2. In the declaration concerning the Arab State, the words "by an Arab in the Jewish State" should be replaced by the words "by a Jew in the Arab State."

ing that no Arab residing in the area of the proposed Arab State shall have the right to opt for citizenship in the proposed Jewish State and no Jews residing in the proposed Jewish State shall have the right to opt for citizenship in the proposed Arab State. The exercise of this right of option will be taken to include the wives and children under eighteen years of age of persons so opting.

Arabs residing in the area of the proposed Jewish State and Jews residing in the area of the proposed Arab State who have signed a notice of intention to opt for citizenship of the other State shall be eligible to vote in the elections to the Constituent Assembly of that State, but not in the elections to the Constituent Assembly of the State in which they reside.

2. *International conventions.* (a) The State shall be bound by all the international agreements and conventions, both general and special, to which Palestine has become a party. Subject to any right of denunciation provided for therein, such agreements and conventions shall be respected by the State throughout the period for which they were concluded.

(b) Any dispute about the applicability and continued validity of international conventions or treaties signed or adhered to by the mandatory Power on behalf of Palestine shall be referred to the International Court of Justice in accordance with the provisions of the Statute of the Court.

3. *Financial obligations.* (a) The State shall respect and fulfil all financial obligations of whatever nature assumed on behalf of Palestine by the mandatory Power during the exercise of the Mandate and recognized by the State. This provision includes the right of public servants to pensions, compensation or gratuities.

(b) These obligations shall be fulfilled through participation in the Joint Economic Board in respect of those obligations applicable to Palestine as a whole, and individually in respect of those applicable to, and fairly apportionable between, the States.

(c) A Court of Claims, affiliated with the Joint Economic Board, and composed of one member appointed by the United Nations, one representative of the United Kingdom and one representative of the State concerned, should be established. Any dispute between the United Kingdom and the States respecting claims not recognized by the latter should be referred to that Court.

(d) Commercial concessions granted in respect of any part of Palestine prior to the adoption of the resolution by the General Assembly shall continue to be valid according to their terms, unless modified by agreement between the concession-holder and the State.

The United Nations Resolution, November 22, 1968

The Security Council,

Expressing its continuing concern with the grave situation in the Middle East;

Emphasizing the inadmissibility of the acquisition of territory by war and the need to work for a just and lasting peace in which every State in the area can live in security;

Emphasizing further that all Member States in their acceptance of the Charter of the United Nations have undertaken to act in accordance with Article 2 of the Charter;

1. Affirms that the fulfillment of Charter principles requires the establishment of a just and lasting peace in the Middle East which should include the application of both the following principles:

    (i) Withdrawal of Israeli armed forces from territories occupied in the recent conflict;

    (ii) Termination of all claims or states of belligerency and respect for and acknowledgement of the sovereignty, territorial integrity and political independence of every State in the area and their right to live in peace within secure and recognized boundaries free from threats or acts of force;

2. Affirms further the necessity

    (a) For guaranteeing freedom of navigation through international waterways in the area;

    (b) For achieving a just settlement of the refugee problem;

    (c) For guaranteeing the territorial inviolability and political independence of every State in the area, through measures including the establishment of demilitarized zones;

3. Requests the Secretary-General to designate a Special Representative to proceed to the Middle East to establish and maintain contacts with the States concerned in order to promote agreement and assist efforts to achieve a peaceful and accepted settlement in accordance with the provisions and principles in this resolution;

4. Requests the Secretary-General to report to the Security Council on the progress of the efforts of the Special Representative as soon as possible.

Arab refugees from territory that became Israel in 1948

Date	Source	Estimate	UNRWA Rolls
1948	Institute Mediterranean Affairs	395,000	960,000
1948	Dr. Ralph Bunche, UN	500,000	960,000
1948	Dr. Walter Pinner, Economic and Social Research Institute, Tel Aviv	539,000	960,000
1948	Israel Government	550,000	960,000
1949	UN Economic Survey	726,000	960,000
1951	UNRWA Census	875,000	904,000
1954	UNRWA Study	757,000	940,000
Sept. 1967	Israeli Census (West Bank & Gaza only)	443,000	628,000

3. Suggested Reading

Albert B. Sabin, et al., The Arabs Need and Want Peace, But..., New York, APPME, 1968. Impressions and conclusions of the Mission of American Professors for Peace in the Middle East.

Fred J. Khouri, The Arab-Israeli Dilemma, Syracuse, Syracuse University Press, 1968. A moderate pro-Arab treatment of the Middle East Crisis.

Morroe Berger, The Arab World Today, New York, Doubleday, 1962. A social scientist's perspective on the forces that shape the contemporary Arab world.

Abba Eban, Never Have Freedom and International Morality Been so Righteously Protected. Text of the address by Israel's Foreign Minister in the General Assembly of the United Nations on June 19, 1967.

Yehuda Gothelf, Israel Today: A New Society in the Making, Tel Aviv, Ihud Olami, 1967. Collection of essays on contemporary Israeli society.

Moshe Dayan, Diary of the Sinai Campaign, New York, Schocken, 1966. An indispensable military history of the 1956 war.

Keesing's Research Report, The Arab-Israeli Conflict: The 1967

Campaign, New York, Scribner's, 1968. A precise day-by-day description of the war.

Jorge Garcia Granada, *The Birth of Israel: The Drama as I Saw It,* New York, Knopf, 1949. A vivid account by a member of the UN Special Committee on Palestine of the work of that committee and subsequent developments.

Robert St. John, *Israel,* New York, Time-Life, 1962. A sympathetic description.

Abraham J. Heschel, *Israel: An Echo of Eternity,* New York, Farrar, Straus & Giroux, 1969. A moving explanation of the spiritual importance of Israel for Jews.

Cecil Roth, *A History of the Jews,* New York, Schocken, 1964. An authoritative work.

Theodor Herzl, *The Jewish State,* New York, Grosset & Dunlap. Blueprint for a state fifty years before its creation, by the father of modern political Zionism.

Arthur Hertzberg, *The Zionist Idea,* New York, Doubleday, 1959 (Atheneum paperback). An historical analysis and reader.

Index